INGRID
BERGMAN

INGRID BERGMAN

JOHN RUSSELL TAYLOR

Photographs from the
KOBAL COLLECTION

ST. MARTIN'S PRESS
New York

Design by Craig Dodd

Library of Congress Catalog Card Number: 83–50765

ISBN 0–312–41796–9

First published in Great Britain by
Elm Tree Books/Hamish Hamilton Ltd

First U.S. Edition

10 9 8 7 6 5 4 3 2 1

CONTENTS

PROLOGUE

It seemed strange, somehow, to hear her speaking Swedish. Of course, you couldn't ever forget that she had been Swedish – along with her near-namesake Ingmar and the long-unglimpsed Garbo, she was certainly the most famous living Swede. But Hollywood does strange things to people and perceptions. Ingrid Bergman the film star was a fictional character, about whom you were told all sorts of things and believed, really believed, very little. So, even knowing that she was Swedish, you did not quite expect her to speak the language, any more than you ever expected Hamlet to speak Danish off-stage. But here, in this film called *Autumn Sonata*, she was playing a Swedish pianist long resident abroad, and doing it with an authority and immediacy that suddenly made you wonder if you had always before seen her through a glass darkly, her quality subtly veiled by the need to conquer an alien language every time.

Maybe the removal of that challenge freed her to accept other, subtler challenges. The challenge, obviously, of working for the first time with Ingmar Bergman, a director she approached with an admiration second only to that she had felt on her first encounter with Roberto Rossellini. The challenge of returning to a Sweden which was seldom kind to its great emigrés, feeling it seemed an overwhelming need to take them down a peg or two – as it had certainly done to Ingrid Bergman on her previous professional returns. (Perhaps she felt a certain relief that this film, though prepared in Sweden, was actually shot in Norway.) And above all, the challenge of playing, as she had seldom done before, a character largely alien to her, a ruthless, self-centred woman who has willingly sacrificed her emotional life to her art.

No one ever accused Ingrid of doing that. In the 1940s it was the most shocking thing – if subsequently, to a newer and more broadminded generation, the most endearing – about her that, at the pinnacle of her profession, she would so readily give it all up for love. But a certain single-minded determination and ruthlessness were not totally alien to her. How could they be, for any film star who had got so far and lasted so long? Even the notorious all-for-love situation with Rossellini arose out of an artistic need, a career decision, and the course it subsequently followed involved an enormous amount of work together which was only by the rather special standards of Hollywood a comedown for her.

The great difference with the role in *Autumn Sonata* was that for once, the first and last time in her film career, Ingrid was playing, with deep understanding and identification, someone who was not, by any stretch of the imagination, a nice woman. George Cukor once told me that he was amazed by Katharine Hepburn in *Suddenly Last Summer*, and said to her afterwards, 'I never knew you could be so evil.' Ingrid in *Autumn Sonata* creates the same sort of surprise. Always before, you knew that this is nice, wholesome, sensible Ingrid Bergman, playing herself in the service of a plot which has been conceived or reconceived to exploit precisely that quality. In *The Visit* there is something different, but there you are aware that this is nice, wholesome, sensible Ingrid Bergman gamely but unsuccessfully trying to convince you that she is a monster of heartlessness and bitterness, inexorably bent on exacting her revenge.

Naturally it helps her, as it helps us, that the *Autumn Sonata* role was written by Ingmar Bergman for Ingrid, not just to exploit qualities the whole world had seen, but to utilise also possibilities which had always been there but never explored by film-makers who saw only the easy way. This woman is a monster – but as presented by the two Bergmans in concert, she is an understandable monster. The only criticism is that we are told all we need to know about the character rather too early in the film. Ingrid plays a pianist – a great pianist, we gather. Her elder daughter, with whom she is staying, has not seen her for seven years, and retains a pathetic, childlike desire to please her and a need for her admiration. This evening, with a little polite urging, she plays for her mother a Chopin prelude. How did the mother like it? Very nice. No, *really*, how did she like it? After a hesitation, the mother sits down herself to play it, explaining how and why she plays it as she does. ('Here tragic, but not maudlin: the emotion is frozen.') And in that scene, one of the finest in all Ingrid's career, we understand exactly how all this woman's love and emotion have been channelled into her music, so that there was none left for husband, daughters, friendship, anything apart from the

Autumn Sonata. *Daughter (Liv Ullmann) plays Chopin while her mother listens. New World Pictures.*

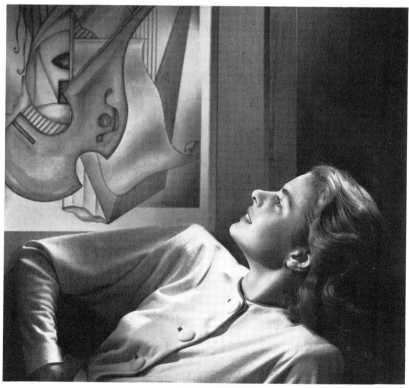

dedicated life of art. Of course she seems cold and self-centred, of course she has been a terrible mother. But this is where her real life is, and only the very hardy would insist without a second thought that it is more important, always, to be a nice person than a great artist.

If there is a need to choose, that is. Ingrid Bergman's rare advantage was that she never seemed to have had to make that choice. No one ever seems to have doubted that she was a nice person. Warm, human, commonsensical, a caring mother, a fiercely loyal friend, a totally professional performer. And yet also a great film star – one of the greatest – and at moments, when necessary, a great actress too. No doubt all performers enjoy performing in some sense: if it is not fun to them, at least it fills an emotional need, and audience response brings satisfaction. But Ingrid quite extraordinarily and obviously enjoyed performing. Ingmar Bergman even suggests that she enjoyed it too much, too patently: this was a quality which had to be kept down, or it could even damage a performance by distracting, making the audience respond to the actress more but the role less.

Perhaps that is true; perhaps it is the key to the very special, personal sort of affection audiences everywhere felt for Ingrid as a woman, as a person. The ability to inspire this is an extraordinary gift, quite apart from the worship inspired by a Garbo, the identification enforced by a Crawford, the edgy, ambiguous feelings provoked by a Davis, the uncomplicated sex appeal of a Harlow. Perhaps the nearest, in this respect strangely enough, was a star who in most other respects could hardly be more different: Marilyn Monroe. Monroe and Bergman had in common a ready way to their audience's heart: whether they were really known or not, correctly understood or not, people felt they knew them, cared about what happened to them as they might about members of their own family or close personal friends. This is a dangerous situation for the loved one to be in, since a deception or betrayal (or what is felt as such) is all the more devastating, all the more difficult for those who love, they do not quite know why, to accept without a violent reaction. At least once in her life Bergman knew the uncomfortable truth of that.

But by the time of *Autumn Sonata* the difficult days were long past. She had been rejected for a while from the ranks of the Hollywood idols, because the whole Rossellini episode seemed to show that this idol had feet of clay. However an idol with feet of clay, though more difficult to worship, may be much easier to love. And after a six-year exile Ingrid had come back even more firmly into the affections of the world. And done it, what is more, on her own terms. Two additional Oscars and other awards aplenty, success on stage such as she could hardly have dreamed possible, another happy marriage – and love unstinted from her public around the world. Now, a return to Sweden and to Swedish, and a peformance which marked a new peak in her career. She had come round full circle. But in another way it was ominously like closing the circle. Already she knew that she had not only been touched by cancer, but that it was continuing to recur and spread. The condition and the treatment made her progressively weaker, so that gradually, little by little, she made her professional farewells and steadfastly prepared herself for death. She was too weak to support an extended run on stage, and she believed that *Autumn Sonata* would be her last film (though as things turned out it was not quite). Some of that feeling seemed to pervade the film itself: it has the air of an actress's testament. And she could hardly have hoped to leave a more extraordinary monument, not only confirming what had always been thought and felt about her, but providing an unexpected new perspective.

In the four years left to her after *Autumn Sonata*, Ingrid did a play and then broke her own rest period to do a television movie about Golda Meir. But she did not hide from herself or from anyone else that the end must soon come. She worked with her old friend Alan Burgess on a semi-autobiography, and slowly but surely put things in order. In a valediction forbidding mourning, she thought back over her career and her life, and tried to see the sense and the pattern in them both. Who knows whether she ever finally succeeded. But for the rest of us the life and its meaning continue to command our attention. For some reason we need to make sense of it all. Probably because she was not just another film star, but someone we loved.

SWEDEN

Whether Ingrid's Swedishness was a complete imaginative reality to her public, it was certainly a physical and emotional reality to her. Her situation at the height of the Rossellini scandal was complicated by her never having become an American citizen, unlike her first husband. When he asked her why, her answer was both simple and mysterious: 'I just know I'm not going to be a happy person being an American when Sweden is still there.' Not a reasonable answer, but one which made sense to her. By her own admission she was always intuitive rather than logical. Most of the worst troubles in her life came from precisely these qualities, but also her basic strengths: as Howard Hughes, of all people, wrote to her on the birth of her first, illegitimate child by Rossellini, her most admirable qualities were 'courage, utter simplicity, and lack of guile or subterfuge.' All of these were clearly with her long before she ever left Sweden.

One could not say that she had a typical Swedish upbringing – or typical anything, come to that. It was, however, in many respects a conventional upbringing, particularly in matters moral and religious. By an odd coincidence, she was not only brought up Lutheran, as one might expect in Sweden, but confirmed and had her first daughter baptised by a pastor also called Bergman, whose son Ingmar was later to find his own fame as an explorer of the tormented Swedish psyche. Tormented Ingrid never seems to have been. The only surviving child of happily married parents, she was born in Stockholm on 29 August 1915. Much later, reading her parents' letters before their marriage, she uncovered the story of their long struggle to get married, over the objections of her mother's parents because her father, Justus Bergman, was felt, as a not notably successful painter, to be insufficiently solid and reliable. It took him seven years of unofficial engagement before he had built up a photographic business sufficiently to convince his prospective German in-laws that he was respectable enough to marry their daughter Friedel.

Justus Bergman seems always to have been expansive, generous, maybe a bit feckless. But Friedel was obviously the determined one who kept him neatly but not too much in check. They had two children who died in infancy, and then, after a gap of seven years, Ingrid came along. Her mother died when she was just three, so she retained no conscious memory of her; instead her father brought her up, with the aid of his unmarried sister Ellen and, later, a young governess called Greta, with whom, in proper romantic film fashion, he fell in love. Again, there was family opposition, this time from his family, his sisters feeling that he should settle to a staid widowhood instead of yearning to marry a girl half his age. All the same, the young Ingrid adored her; she adored her strict Aunt Ellen; and above all she adored her father. She seems, then as later, to have had an almost infinite capacity for adoration.

And indeed, Justus Bergman sounds to have been just the sort of father any daughter would adore. Jolly, generous, full of rather fantastic dreams, when he was not letting Ingrid take what money she wanted from a handful of coins (this shocked her already frugal nature: parents were supposed to be strict about children's pocket money), he was urging her to become an opera-singer – now that was a nice glamorous, colourful profession. Obviously her complete devotion to her father was going to shape all her subsequent relations with men; just as his death from cancer when she was thirteen was going to leave indelible marks on her personality and attitude to life. Especially since it was followed six months later by the death of her Aunt Ellen, in Ingrid's arms, from a heart attack. These two deaths thrust her into the apparently happy but much less prosperous, more strictly run household of her Aunt Hilda and Uncle Otto, with their five children. They also no doubt contributed to making her a withdrawn, painfully shy teenager, who blushed at the slightest provocation, was embarrassed by her considerable height and habitually fell over her large feet. Her only release was into a world of fantasy and later, as she discovered at school, an unexpected ability to externalize that fantasy, to act things out on any makeshift stage when she could magically become something or someone outside her own ungainly self.

Thus, unexpectedly, the actress was born. When Ingrid confided her ambition to her cousins their reaction was an unceremonious: 'How can you? You're so awkward.' But even then she had her own brand of stubbornness and determination. While she agreed docilely enough she would go to secretarial school, as her Uncle Otto thought sensible, if she failed to get into acting school, at least she was going to give herself the chance to fail first. She applied to audition for entry to the Royal Dramatic School when she was seventeen, and very seriously, as though her life depended on it – after all she felt it did – set about preparing the required extracts to show off her various possibilities as an actress, or actress-to-be. She already had her own ideas on this subject, concluding cannily that since most of the applicants would be showing themselves off in strong drama, it would be good to be different and even, if possible, make the judges laugh. Her drama teacher suggested a scene from a Hungarian play, in which the bold peasant girl is flirting with and teasing a shy boy, and makes her entrance with a flying leap, demanding attention. Her back-up piece was something quieter, again making use of her height and her skinny, still-boyish figure – an extract from Rostand's play about Napoleon's son, *L'Aiglon*.

Came the day of the audition. Ingrid was ready with her impersonation of the flirtatious Hungarian peasant-girl. At a given signal, she bounded on to stage, stood there and delivered her first line. Then she glanced down at the judges and froze. They were chattering among themselves, paying no attention whatever. She hesitated, completely thrown, muffed her second line, and before she could pull herself together and continue was mortified to hear them call, 'All right, thank you. Next!' According to her own account, she was so upset by this evident and total failure that she rushed out of the theatre and seriously contemplated ending it all by throwing herself into the harbour, though then sensibly restrained herself with the thought that, the harbour being all cluttered with garbage as it was, this would hardly constitute a desirably decorative and Ophelia-like consummation. (The mixture of high romance and basic practicality at least sounds totally characteristic.) So instead she went glumly home, to find a telephone message that a young friend of hers, also auditioning, had passed the first stage, and so, he said, had she. Madly she rushed back to the theatre to pick up the longed-for white envelope, floated through the second stage of the auditions, then the third (a scene from Strindberg's *Dream Play*), and in the autumn of 1933 began her studies at the Royal Dramatic School, which was at that time the ultimate point of her thinking and her ambition.

But why had the judges been so rudely inattentive? Years later she found out. The famous Swedish director Alf Sjöberg was, it turned out, one of the jury, and eventually Ingrid had the chance to ask him why she had been selected if they thought so little of her. He was amazed. On the contrary, he said, as soon as she leapt on the stage they recognized her astonishing presence, her confidence, that extra something she had which was beyond dispute. Why, they were asking themselves, need they waste precious time seeing any more when she was so obviously right? Perhaps it was fortunate that she did not know this earlier, or it might have turned her head. But it seems unlikely that it would, in the sense of making her over-confident and careless of tuition. She was so ecstatic already at the very idea of really being there, really acting, that she had to keep pinching herself to believe that it was true.

It was, anyway, already built into her puritanical Swedish nature to suppose that pleasures had to be paid for. Very early in her career at the school, confirmation of this occurred when Alf Sjöberg remembered the girl who had so impressed him at the auditions and thought that, even though (or perhaps because) still unformed, she would be perfect for an important subsidiary role in a play he was then casting. Ingrid was naturally thrilled to be appearing already on a professional stage, working with famous actors like Lars Hanson and Inga Tidblad, but did not realize the intensity of resentment this would cause among her contemporaries and seniors at the school. The school's director, Olof Molander, did, but gave in to Sjöberg's insistence. Unfortunately after two days' rehearsals feelings ran so high at the school that Ingrid was physically attacked; Molander had to bow to it and insist that she withdraw from the cast. She was, of course, extremely upset, but at least it taught her a hard but valuable lesson about the bureaucratic structure of the school and its attitudes.

Even so, she always looked back on her days at school as a period of almost unalloyed pleasure. She just loved acting, finding in it a perfect release from all her inhibitions. Throughout her career this same simple delight in the process of acting was to shine through her work – even sometimes to a dangerous degree: when Ingmar Bergman was working with her on *Autumn Sonata* he noted that, 'Sometimes in her profession she puts on masks which do not fit her very well, for she likes so much to play. She enjoys it so much that you can see she enjoys it, and that, in part, is not good.' It was something that maybe acting school should have knocked out of her, though one would hesitate to say that any training should deliberately set out to spoil a trainee's enjoyment of his craft. Possibly if she had continued longer at school and had more early experience on the stage, as was her conscious goal at the time, she might have learnt to wear her professional masks with more ease. And if she had, she might never have become a film star at all, or at any rate the kind of film star she did, for whom the ability to let the personality shine through any mask a particular role requires is of paramount importance.

In this, as in so many parts of her life, fate was rapidly to take a hand. She had, quite by accident, had her earliest first-hand experience of film-making a couple of years before, at the age of fifteen, when she ran into Greta, her ex-governess and her father's last love, to discover that she, a natural beauty, was working quite regularly as a movie extra. Since Ingrid longed to penetrate the mysteries of a film studio and find out how films were made, Greta got her a day's work as an extra. She turned up first thing in the morning, was made up, and at ten a couple of shots were taken of her and some other girls doing their best to look cold and miserable. Then, by 10.15, they were told they could go. Ingrid was disappointed: was that all? But she realized that if she kept her makeup on no one would question her presence there, as they would assume she was waiting to do something else. So she stayed on all day, going from set to set and observing the whole process. When she finally picked up her ten kronor for the day's work she could hardly believe that she had actually been paid for spending the most magical day of her life.

At drama school there was a slight tendency to be snobbish about films: these were not real acting, not like on stage. But Ingrid felt this very little, if at all. At the end of her first year, when most of her contemporaries went off for the summer on a package tour to study Russian theatre, she stayed behind in Stockholm and began to plague her florist uncle Gunnar to see if he could use any of his show-business connections and get her back into films, as an extra, playing small parts, anything. . . . He had a word with a regular customer of his, the actress Karin Swanstrom, who was artistic director of Svenskfilmindustri; she met Ingrid and was sufficiently impressed to arrange for a screen test there and then. It was directed by the leading Swedish film-

maker of that time, Gustav Molander, the brother of the director of the Royal Drama School. And he saw at once, beyond the inevitable gaucheness of the fledgling actress, something extraordinary.

Which was more than Ingrid did. When she saw her test, and realized for the first time how she looked in motion, on screen, she was painfully unimpressed. Not, however, discouraged: her first thought, which she artlessly confided to Molander, was: 'If I did more, I could be better later.' All through her career she remained the same: however good she was, however satisfied her director, she always thought she could be better on the next take. In her early days in Swedish movies they even nicknamed her 'Better-later'. However, Molander and Karin Swanstrom thought she was good enough right now, at any rate for a small role as the romantic interest for one of a group of young bohemians in search of a good time in a film called *Munkbrogreven* (*The Count of Monks Bridge*), which happened to be shooting that summer. She played a maid in a sleazy hotel where the young men stop off in their day's search to evade Sweden's then stringent liquor laws, and is first glimpsed on screen struggling into a boldly striped dress so that she can rush to the window and wave at her beloved, Edvin Adolphson, who was also co-director of the film. It was not – nor was it intended to be – the kind of role or the kind of film which would automatically launch a major star. But it was a start, and she was noticed: the critics found charm and freshness in her work, even if they were rather liable to characterize her as 'somewhat overweight' or even 'hefty'.

After this experience Ingrid would probably have gone back quite happily to drama school that autumn. But everyone connected with her film debut urged otherwise: she was immediately offered a contract which guaranteed her 5,000 kronor miminum the first year, with annual increments of 1,000 kronor for two further years, plus payment for special private lessons in voice-production, dancing and movement, the possibility of theatre work, and various fringe benefits. It was an offer difficult for an eighteen-year-old actress to refuse. But she might possibly have refused it if Olof Molander had not taken such a strong line with her, forbidding her to leave the Royal Dramatic School before she had completed her courses. Even at this stage, Ingrid was extremely stubborn and self-confident in everything connected with her career: decidedly not a person to be bullied. On her first film she had distinguished herself by arguing with her director all along the way and actually taking over unbidden to instruct the much older and more experienced comedienne Tollie Zellman in how to wrap fish. And when Olof Molander started commanding her she at once dug her heels in. Who was he, anyway, to be so superior about movies?

Also, the movie then being set up, *Branningar* (*Ocean Breakers*) was to be her first starring role. Strong stuff, too, requiring her to be beautiful, noble, self-sacrificing, and bear an illegitimate

child. A rather idiotically melodramatic confection, the film
concerns an unwilling Lutheran minister who is carried away by
lust on sighting Ingrid, a local fisherman's daughter, and then
promptly gets struck by lightning and suffers from a convenient
bout of amnesia while she bears his child and tells no one who the
father is. It all comes out right in the end when the minister
recovers his memory, confesses his sins to his congregation, and
leaves the ministry to become a farmer and marry the girl.
Despite its manifold sillinesses, it was a good beginning for a new
star, who got excellent notices, both for her beauty and for some
hints of acting ability, or at least a brand of natural sincerity
which carried her with dignity and conviction through her all-
too-conventional role.

But more important was the connection already established
between Ingrid and Gustav Molander, far and away the most
distinguished and capable director then working in the Swedish
cinema, since the death of Stiller and the retirement from direction
of the other great figure from the silent period, Victor Sjöstrom.
Molander had had Ingrid in mind as his leading lady ever since
directing the first test, and after *Branningar* had been completed
he was ready to put his plans into practice. He was eventually to
direct six of the ten films she made in Sweden before settling
definitively in America, and he had a long-term strategy in mind.
In his first film with her, *Swedenhielms*, she plays the second
female lead, the principal feminine role going to her discoverer and
mentor Karin Swanstrom. The film is based on a play by the third
great Bergman in Swedish drama, Hjalmar, about the complicated
family situation of an unworldly Swedish scientist called
Swedenhielm, whose household is held together by his long-
suffering sister-in-law and housekeeper Marta (Karin Swanstrom).
One of his sons is engaged to a rich young woman (Ingrid
Bergman) but hesitates to marry her, as it might seem, for money.
There is a problem with money-lenders and forged IOUs, and
each of the sons is suspected successively, but in the end Marta
admits that she falsified the signatures to keep the household
going, and all ends happily. Ingrid again got good notices and
made a favourable impression, without yet having to carry a film
all by herself.

Probably the most significant thing about *Swedenhielms* for her
was working with its star, Gösta Ekman. Even when nearly
twenty, Ingrid seems to have remained emotionally quite unformed and unguarded. We can judge of her reactions at this time
very directly by the published extracts from a sort of professional
diary she then kept, the thick leather-bound volume with a
locking metal clasp and her name engraved on the cover, given
her by her Uncle Gunnar when she was fourteen. Her reactions to
Gösta Ekman, though obviously innocent and platonic, are those
of a lovelorn schoolgirl: 'The man I looked up to as a god on
earth. . . . It was as if I had known him all my life; as if he was
my father, he inspired me in a very mystical way . . . I wonder if

he feels how my eyes follow him like a dog. I adore him more than ever.'

The comparison with her father is a gift to the amateur psycho-analyst. All through her life Ingrid was attracted to older men, figures of authority, as though to replace the beloved father she had lost too soon. Not that she was any weakling herself: Joe Steele, her longtime publicist and friend, sums the situation up in his book *Ingrid Bergman: An Intimate Portrait* (1959) as 'a strong woman in search of a stronger man.' And while she herself readily recognized that she was generally decisive and self-willed in everything connected with her career, in all other respects she was liable to depend, to an almost pathetic degree, on the rulings of the men in her life. Gösta Ekman was the great male star in Sweden during the Thirties, and even a spectacularly beautiful beginner like Ingrid could hardly have imagined herself as a suitable consort, so her feelings remained on the high, ideal plane of hero-worship. Nonetheless, the pattern of behaviour they indicate was to remain consistent with her for the rest of her life, and was at the root of most of her personal tragedies as well as her triumphs.

Her next film again saw her playing second female lead, while the more mature and established Karin Carlsson got all the big juicy dramatic scenes. In *Valborgsmassoafton* (*Walpurgis Night*) Karin Carlsson was a wife fearful of childbearing who has an abortion, shoots a blackmailer and eventually kills herself; Ingrid was merely the husband's loyal, patient secretary (secretly in love with him, of course) who is still around to pick up the pieces at the end of the film. The object of her mute adoration was Lars Hanson, a former co-star of Garbo's, and her father in the film was played by the great Victor Sjöstrom, now content just to act. She was with Lars Hanson and Karin Swanstrom again in her next film, directed by Molander and called *Pa Solsidan* (*On the Sunny Side*). This time, at last, she plays the central character and gets top female billing, as a beautiful young orphaned bank clerk who is wooed by a dashing young writer (Edvin Adolphson), but won by a relatively conservative landowner who then worries that she may find him and country life stodgy, goes through some agonies of jealousy over whether she still finds the writer attract-ive, but finally discovers that the writer is in fact in love with his sister, so all ends happily. It is all a charming, lightweight confection, and followed *Swedenhielms* to some international success and a prompt American showing. *Variety* found Ingrid 'pretty and capable, rating a Hollywood berth' and the *New York Times* enthused about her 'natural charm' which by itself made the film worth a visit.

Clearly by now, in 1936, Ingrid's progress was beginning to accelerate. Not only professionally, for about this time she had become engaged to a handsome young dentist she had met a couple of years previously, Petter Lindstrom. She was twenty and he was twenty-nine: he was a strong, determined, rather old-

Opposite top. Valborgsmassoafton (Walpurgis Night), *with* (left) *Victor Sjöstrom and (right) Gustav Edgren, directing. Svenskfilmindustri.*
Opposite bottom. With Aino Tavbo in the same film. Svenskfilmindustri.

Opposite. Pa Solsidan (On the Sunny Side). *Svenskfilmindustri.*

fashioned young man, who fitted in well with the father-figure image that she seemed to require. Perhaps too well, since she was bound to change and grow in the next few years, while he was already fixed in his ways and sure of his standards. But at this point he seemed to be just the steadying influence she needed, ready to assist in career decisions, advise and back her up in all areas of life. In fact most people around them, relatives and professional colleagues alike, clearly regarded them as an ideal couple, and predicted nothing but good of their marriage, which took place on 10 July 1937.

Before that, Ingrid had taken what proved to be the most important single step in her Swedish career, when she co-starred with Gösta Ekman in an original screen story specially written for them by Gustav Molander and directed by him: *Intermezzo*. In it Ekman plays a world-famous violinist, happily married and with three children he adores. But on to the scene comes Ingrid, an aspiring young pianist who is teaching his daughter to play. The violinist is struck by her talent as well as her beauty and gives her some encouragement which is at first purely professional; then gradually, unwillingly, they slip into a passionate affair. This continues while they go on a concert tour of Europe together, but finally she realizes she must give him up for his own good, release him to return to wife and family. The 'intermezzo' is over, and she goes on to develop her own career and become . . . well, quite possibly to become the pianist Ingrid was to play in

Below. With Lars Hanson in the same film. Svenskfilmindustri.

Autumn Sonata, back in Sweden forty-two years later.

It did not, and does not, seem like much more than a routine weepie, if made with a little more style than usual. But it was an ideal showcase for Ingrid's special gifts of passionate sincerity, directness and warmth, and incidentally put to cunning use her schoolgirl idolization of Gösta Ekman, which shines through their scenes together. It got her better notices in Sweden than ever before, and made her beyond question the country's top female attraction. Later Molander said of it: 'I created *Intermezzo* for her, but I was not responsible for its success. Ingrid herself made it successful through her performance. The truth is, nobody discovered her. Nobody launched her. She discovered herself.' But through that self-discovery came other discoveries, which were to lead to America, Hollywood and the most radical change in her whole life.

Not all at once, however. Right away, she made her somewhat delayed debut on stage, in a frenzy of nerves which nevertheless led to a major hit with the second production, a Hungarian comedy also directed by Molander. She married and starred in another Molander film based on another Hjalmar Bergman play, *Dollar*, a comedy with a very complicated plot about three married couples, all six of whom suspect their respective spouses of dalliance, in all cases quite without justification. In this for the first time film critics discovered that, given half a chance, she could play comedy admirably: not only was her appearance

Opposite. Dollar. *Svenskfilmindustri*.

Below. Intermezzo, *the Swedish version, with Gösta Ekman*. *Svenskfilmindustri*.

Above. Dollar. *Svenskfilmindustri.*

Left. With George Rydeberg in Dollar. *Svenskfilmindustri.*

'lustrous', but her comic timing 'superb'. To ring the changes, her next film with Molander was a strong drama, *En Kvinnas Ansikte* (*A Woman's Face*), better remembered these days from the American remake of the same name, with Joan Crawford playing Ingrid's role of a woman embittered by facial disfigurement who becomes a new person after an operation makes her beautiful. Unashamed melodrama, the Swedish version was remarkable mainly for Molander's heavy reliance on Ingrid's good sense and instinct to resolve plot problems: while he hesitated over the ending, where the heroine has somehow to pay the price for changing her mind and shooting her former accomplice in a kidnap attempt on a little boy in her charge, Ingrid was quite certain she should go on trial and the conclusion be left to the audience.

That and the fact that Ingrid, for the first but by no means the last time in her long career, believed in the film and fought for her role in it, against the advice of her bosses. Confident, in this specific area, almost to pushiness, she dismissed the subject Svenskfilmindustri wanted her to make, *En Enda Natt* (*Only One Night*) as garbage, and agreed to do it only as a trade-off: they let her do *A Woman's Face*, and she would do their foolish yarn in exchange. In this instance she was undoubtedly right. *A Woman's*

Below. En Kvinnas Ansikte (A Woman's Face). *Svenskfilmindustri.*

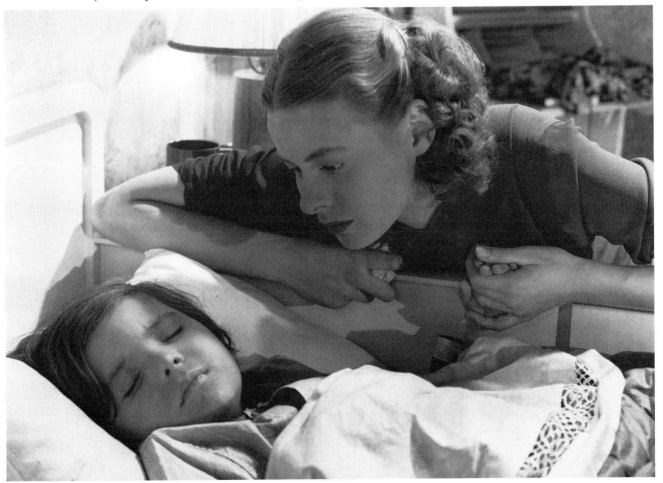

Opposite. Portrait from En Kvinnas Ansikte (A Woman's Face). *Svenskfilmindustri.*

Right. En Enda Natt (Only One Night). *Svenskfilmindustri.*

Face, if difficult to take very seriously, at least provides a good, showy role for an actress, and Ingrid handles it more than adequately. *Only One Night*, on the other hand, is a load of outdated nonsense about a rough young circus attendant raised to the heights when a rich aristocrat recognizes him as his illegitimate son, but finally realizing that he has not the breeding to live up to his new place in society. Worse, all Ingrid has to do is be ladylike as the classy young woman who does not fancy the bastard heir and is relieved when he returns to his coarser love back in the circus. Even Molander's direction could not salvage much from that. But *A Woman's Face* remains exceptional as an example of Ingrid's judgement in the choice of material proving correct: more often than not she fought like a tiger for the wrong roles and was resistant or hesitant to the right roles even when they dropped right in her lap.

By the beginning of 1938 the wheels were in motion for her major move out of Sweden. But though she already recognized the limitations of her position in Sweden as those of a big fish in a small pond, she was as yet unaware that in the States David O. Selznick had issued instructions to his East Coast representative Kay Brown to go and look at this new Swedish film *Intermezzo* to check if it was a subject worth acquiring for a remake. One foreign offer was already dangling, though: she was given a screen test by UFA in Berlin, and, when they found that satisfactory, offered a three-picture contract. She would be acting in German, her mother's language, and have the chance to build a new reputation abroad. With her husband's approval, she accepted and set off to make the first of the three films, *Die Vier Gesellen* (*The Four Companions*) even though already pregnant. It was a lightweight comedy-drama directed by Carl Froelich, about

Below. Die Vier Gesellen (The Four Companions). *On location in Berlin with Sabine Peters, Ursula Herking and Carsta Lock. UFA.*

four business-girls in a design partnership and their tangles with life and love: when it came out most people found it plodding and longwinded.

But some time before that Ingrid was quite clear in her own mind that she did not particularly want to complete the contract it if could be avoided – even though the next role designed for her by UFA, that of Charlotte Corday, was one she would very much like to play. Germany was certainly a bigger pond than Sweden, though by no means so big as Hollywood. And Hollywood, should an acceptable offer come, had the advantage that the only Swede spectacularly installed, Garbo, was now playing roles very different from what might come the way of the young Ingrid, while Germany already had two big female stars from Sweden. Zarah Leander was cast generally in the Garbo mould, but Kristina Söderbaum was much of an age and a type with

Below. With Hans Sohnker in Die Vier Gesellen (The Four Companions). *UFA.*

Ingrid, and in addition happened to be married to the important German director Veit Harlan. Still, it is difficult to imagine, even had things been otherwise, Ingrid playing Kristina Söderbaum's role in *Jew Süss*. Always the least political of women, she knew little of the Nazi rule in Germany when she went to film there. But, trusting as always to her instincts, she soon began to find herself very uncomfortable, enveloped in an atmosphere of fear and mistrust. She did not see why she should be so eager to

Below. Ingrid as a healthy Teutonic pin-up. Atelier Binder/UFA.

Atelier Binder, Berlin phot.

Ingrid Bergma

„Ross" Verlag

A 2244/1
„Ross" Verlag

Ingrid Bergman

Reproduction verboten

kowtow to Goebbels if he invited her to tea, and the repeated assurance that it was only because he had a soft spot for pretty young actresses did not make her feel much better about it. Fortunately the crunch never came, though she knew even as it was that her sturdy independence and refusal to give the Nazi salute on public occasions made those around her nervous. As her pregnancy become more evident, the company speeded up shooting on her remaining scenes, and she was able to get back to Sweden in good time to give birth to her daughter Pia, after a brief visit to Paris with Petter, in the autumn of 1938.

By that time, anyway, one needed no special prescience to know that trouble was brewing in Europe. And it was by no means certain that Sweden would wish, or be able, to stay out of it. That was not yet an immediate concern, but it was something to be borne in mind as Ingrid, her husband and her agent mulled over the various offers received from abroad, from Britain and more especially America. Not only was it time professionally that she should look for larger horizons than Sweden could offer; it might very soon become the best way out of a Europe thrown into chaos by war, for Ingrid and her baby, and possibly her husband too. The trouble with most of the offers from America was that they were disquietingly vague: term contracts, with options, from Paramount, RKO and Fox, but nothing concrete about roles. For all Ingrid knew, on any of them she might sit in Hollywood kicking her heels for months with nothing to do. And in any case she would have no say in what sort of role the studio might wish on her. It was definitely not good enough as an alternative to her assured position in the Swedish cinema.

But something different, and far more specific, was on its way. Though when Kay Brown went to see *Intermezzo* she thought that the story of the film was neither here nor there, she was knocked sideways by the charisma of its leading lady. And told Selznick so in no uncertain terms. Even though Ingrid had been getting enthusiastic notices from the New York critics for a couple of years, Los Angeles is another world entirely. Selznick had never even heard of her, and even after he had looked at the film for himself and decided to negotiate to bring its leading lady to Hollywood he was not entirely sure whether she was not Gösta Stevens (the male scriptwriter) instead. However, such muddles were sorted out (in Hollywood they were not used to mere writers getting such prominent billing) and Kay Brown dispatched to London and then Stockholm with an offer. This time it was for a routine seven-year contract, but also, more encouraging, for a specific role: the same she had played in the Swedish *Intermezzo*, but in an American remake opposite Leslie Howard.

When Kay Brown arrived in Stockholm Ingrid had just given birth to Pia, and her family situation with Petter seemed so fine and uncomplicated that Kay Brown had pangs of conscience about even trying to take her away from all this. But though Petter was against the seven-year contract, he proved surprisingly to be very much for the one film: why didn't she sign just for that, and then both she and Selznick would have a fair chance to see what happened. He would stay in Sweden, and his mother would look after Pia while Ingrid was away. If she had any qualms, his attitude must have resolved them. For Ingrid subsequently described her situation with him as one of almost total dependence.

He so tied me down by being helpful that for the rest of my life I've been helpless without a man to tell me what to do. Except when I'm doing my own work, that is. When I'm on stage, or in front of that camera, nobody can tell me anything except the director, because I know instinctively what to do, and how, I think, to do it. But in my private life, if anyone asks, 'Do you

Below and opposite. Hollywood beginnings: Intermezzo *with Leslie Howard. Selznick International- United Artists.*

want this room or that room?' I don't care. Or, 'Would you like fish or meat?' I don't know. It's not important to me . . . Men in my life taught me to be dependent, beginning with my father, and after that Uncle Otto, who didn't want me to become an actress, and then Petter, even before our engagement. Not that it was Petter's fault. I was the one who asked him for advice and help in those early days.

So, with Petter's approval, she went – but strictly on the conditions he approved of. On 6 May 1939 she arrived in New York on board the 'Queen Mary'. Three months later almost to the day she was setting off home on the 'Queen Mary', with no idea when or whether she would ever be back. Everything seemed to have gone well, but the film would not be premiered until later in the

year, and then everyone would see. Meanwhile, there were the
threads of her family life to take up, a newly purchased house to
get used to, and another Swedish film to do, *Juninatten* (*A June
Night*), a romantic melodrama about a young dispenser who
nearly dies when accidentally shot by her suicidal lover but
survives to find the right young man second time around. It was
not up to much, though it had a respectable success in Sweden.
But it hardly mattered, since by then two things had happened:
Intermezzo, American-style, had opened, and the Second World
War had begun. Not necessarily in that order of importance.

Above. Juninatten (A June Night).
Svenskfilmindustri.

AMERICA

In America she was to meet many strong men, and love and depend on them all, in varying ways and to varying degrees. Selznick, Victor Fleming, Spencer Tracy, Gary Cooper, Alfred Hitchcock. . . . And later and most, Roberto Rossellini, though, the mountain coming to Mohammed, she had to go to Italy in search of him. And yet, in some ways, it always seems more like an excuse than a reason for anything. Ingrid was, as she never tired of pointing out, even if others failed to do so, a big woman – physically strong, professionally secure, self-centred (for good and ill), passionate, wilful and inclined, unless someone bullied her right back, to be domineering. She always knew what was right, what was best for her – even when she patently didn't. Maybe she was in certain respects the silly, dependent creature she liked to picture herself. But they must have been fairly unimportant respects, or she would hardly have ended up, as she did, one of the tutelary deities of Women's Lib, a trail-blazer in moral freedom and independent lifestyle. Possibly she cried all the way to the head of the column, but she got there anyway, and that is what finally counts.

We need only consider her relations with her first American strong man, David O. Selznick, to see that. When she got to New York that first time she was met by Kay Brown, and given a couple of weeks to brush up her English, which proved alarmingly to be English English, so that she found the American variety (or varieties) disturbingly hard to follow. A crash course in current theatre, beginning with *Tobacco Road*, did not help much with that little problem, but almost before she knew it she was being whisked off by train to Los Angeles. What she did not know then was the amount of time and trouble her producer was devoting to the vital question of just how she should be reworked before she could be burst upon the great American public. That she had to be reworked no one doubted. New name (unless the old one proved to be immensely valuable abroad), new eyebrows, new teeth, new hair-colour and so ad infinitum. Meanwhile, her great worry was actually getting to meet Selznick. After a number of boss shots (he was rather occupied at the time with a little opus called *Gone With the Wind*), she finally ran him to earth guzzling in Miriam Hopkins's kitchen. He proceeded to throw at her a list of proposed changes. She proceeded to tell him in no uncertain terms that he must have made a mistake with her, and if he wanted to change everything she might just as well take the train back to Sweden this minute.

That, it would seem, was how Selznick's great idea dawned on him. Get publicity by avoiding publicity, change nothing about her, and sell her as the anti-star star, the first true natural in Hollywood. Not only was that the easiest way of dealing with this intransigent new acquisition, but it also made a sense which appealed to the practised showman in Selznick. A surprise was always saleable. But also, he clearly recognized from the start that this youthful-looking twenty-three-year-old innocent from

Sweden was not going to be exactly a pushover for any modifications he might suggest. And he was sure that he was really on to something. A big, important star in the years to come who might as well be nurtured now. It may even have occurred to him already that she could be very profitable to him indirectly even if he never dealt personally with her again: every artist under contract could be sold, bartered or somehow traded off, and as the 1940s wore on it sometimes seemed that Selznick was more interested in this kind of horse-trading than in actually making movies.

However, for the moment the main thing was to get this show on the road. He quarrelled with the first director of the new *Intermezzo*, William Wyler, on the first day of shooting, and instead Ingrid was assigned the eccentric Russian Gregory Ratoff, whose own brand of fractured English made hers sound like Anna Neagle. Anyway, she had her own English coach now, a closet Swede (as later emerged) called Ruth Roberts, who tactfully steered her round following Ratoff's readings of the lines too precisely. Also, the film was familiar ground, and her co-stars, Leslie Howard as the violinist and Edna Best as his slighted wife, were both highly professional and unselfishly helpful to the newcomer. Everyone was impressed by her stamina and zeal in pursuing perfection: aided by the fact that she could play the

Below. Selznick's Golden Girl.
United Artists.

piano a bit, she went so far as to make herself note-perfect on the concerto she had to be seen playing in the film. She had to be patient, since Selznick was as much a stickler for details as she was herself, and kept on shooting and reshooting her first entrance (a reaction shot as she watches the violinist playing with his daughter at the piano) so that it would somehow be stunning and say everything necessary about the new star in seconds. They were still doing it, just one more time, right up to the moment of her departure, so that she just barely caught her train.

Selznick certainly filled the bill as a substitute father, even if he let her have her own way in most things. He was always available for consultation on problems, however trivial, and though his criticisms were often hard they were always just, and actuated by the same motives as her own work: to get everything as near perfection as was humanly possible. If she did not fall in love with him even a little bit, that was probably because as her first American he remained deeply strange to her, and because his wife, Irene Selznick, became at once and remained one of her closest and dearest friends. She was hardly back in Sweden, it seemed, when the film opened and had an enormous success world-wide. A star was definitely born, and Selznick would not wait to exercise his option for another picture – all that Petter had prudently permitted her to agree to. As the war spread over Europe and she completed *Juninatten*, he ordered her back to Hollywood in no uncertain terms – preferably with husband and child.

It was already getting difficult to cross the Atlantic, but by 31 December 1939 Ingrid and Pia were in Genoa waiting to take ship for New York on the first of the New Year; Petter, who had come to see them off, felt it was his duty to remain in Sweden, in case it got involved in the war, and he and Ingrid had a melancholy parting at the New Year's dance, uncertain that they would ever see each other again. Good news reached Ingrid by cable during the voyage: she was to tell reporters in New York that the first film projected for her was about Joan of Arc, her favourite historical heroine. When she arrived this instruction was countermanded, and it soon emerged that Selznick had no immediate plans for her. Though it was agreeable to be in the relative safety of New York with her child, she could never bear inactivity for long, so she began to nudge Selznick, gently, about finding her something to do. If the story of Joan of Arc was tactless, showing as it did the present allies England and France at each other's throats, there must surely be something less political.

And very soon something suitable emerged, from a totally unexpected direction. The stage producer Vinton Freedley was planning a production of Molnar's play *Liliom* (later famed chiefly as the basis of the Rodgers-and-Hammerstein musical *Carousel*), starring Burgess Meredith in the title role of the fairground busker who is sent back after death to intervene for good in the life of his wife and daughter. And he thought Ingrid might be interested in joining the production. She read the play, and got the surprise of her life when she discovered that Freedley wanted her for the female lead. She and Kay Brown ('two strong women,' she says) managed to wear down Selznick's resistance to the idea, and she duly began to brush up her English and learn the role. At the first rehearsal it was Vinton Freedley's turn to get the surprise of his life, when he discovered that Ingrid was not Signe Hasso, another Swedish emigré then in Hollywood, and a far more experienced stage actress. Fortunately, despite his wails of horror at having signed the wrong girl, he decided it was too late to do anything about it, Ingrid got on famously with her elfin co-star (even though he was a head shorter than her), and when the play opened they both got rave reviews. Even Molnar, notoriously difficult to please, opined that she was perfect.

The play successfully ran its appointed two months, and then Ingrid found herself almost exactly where she had been before: in New York, waiting for a summons to work in Hollywood which seemed no nearer to coming. At least Petter came out to visit her and Pia, but to her distress he did not like New York at all, being unable to see the glamour for the grime. It was only a short stay: now that it seemed clear Sweden would not be

Opposite. In Rage in Heaven *being menaced by Robert Montgomery. C. S. Bull/MGM.*

Below. Adam had Four Sons. *Columbia.*

Opposite. Ingrid as the brassy barmaid in Dr Jekyll and Mr Hyde. *MGM.*

involved in the war, Petter had decided to come to America for good, but he had to go back and sort things out in Sweden first. After a summer in the East, Ingrid decided to go to Hollywood off her own bat, on the principle that her presence there might force Selznick to do something for her. And so it did. Not St Joan, as she continued to hope, but a couple of loan-outs to other studios.

Neither was very thrilling. In *Adam Had Four Sons*, directed again by Gregory Ratoff, she played a long-suffering French governess (why French is not clear, except on the convenient Hollywood assumption that all foreign accents are indistinguishable) who looks after a family of men through trials and tribulations when the mother dies, until at last the father recognizes that he loves her, after she has been carrying a torch for him for half a lifetime. (An oddly similar situation, Ingrid may have reflected, to that in her own family after her mother's death.) In *Rage in Heaven*, made at MGM within striking distance of Garbo, whom Ingrid never at this point got to meet, she played the long-suffering wife of a psychopathic Robert Montgomery, who is insanely jealous of her throughout and finally stages his own suicide in such a way as to frame George Sanders, his main possible rival, for his murder. Again, Ingrid seemed to be the part of each film best liked by critics and public; people started saying

Below. Dr Jekyll's dream image of Ivy. MGM.

what a waste it was that Hollywood did not appear to have much idea how to use her. And she herself was getting tired of smiling through her sufferings: she wanted a role she could really get her teeth into.

That materialized unexpectedly when Victor Fleming wanted her, still at MGM, for his new version of *Doctor Jekyll and Mr Hyde*, with Spencer Tracy in the title role(s). Naturally she was to be cast as the good girl, Jekyll's long-suffering fiancée, while Lana Turner was to play the tarty barmaid Hyde turns to and savages. Once she had read the script, though, Ingrid had other ideas. Why did not she and Lana exchange roles? Casting against type for both of them would be interesting and provocative. She even forced Fleming into secretly making a test of her as the brassy but ultimately pathetic Ivy: something stars definitely did not do in class-conscious Hollywood. She then had ammunition to counter Selznick's objections, and get things to go the way she wanted them, to everybody's ultimate satisfaction: at least she had had the opportunity to show she was an actress and did not always have to be a sweet nonentity. Of course, the essential niceness was still visible: Ivy is more pathetic beneath her shameless exterior than 'evil', as contemporary critics claimed. But it was certainly a new side of Ingrid to be seen on screen.

She continued to explore a similar vein in a stage production Selznick had set up in Santa Barbara, largely one suspects to placate her, as part of a short-lived summer theatre enterprise. It was what might be regarded as a natural for her, treading for once directly in the footsteps of Garbo: Eugene O'Neill's *Anna Christie*, in which she had to play a prostitute who comes home to her Swedish sea-captain father and determines to redeem herself through the love of a good man. The production was successful enough to go on to San Francisco and New Jersey before she had to return to Hollywood to make another film. She hoped it would be *For Whom the Bell Tolls*. After all, had not Ernest Hemingway himself confided to *Life* magazine that he saw her as the ideal choice for the role of Maria, a Spanish guerilla who has a passionate affair with an American idealist fighting for the Republican cause in the Spanish Civil War? But unfortunately Hemingway's say-so was not enough for Paramount, the company that owned the property: they were determined to cast a new discovery of their own, the Norwegian dancer Vera Zorina. There seemed to be nothing Hemingway or Selznick could do to make them change their mind, so with the role denied her, Ingrid made the best of a bad job. Petter had finally come over to live in America, arriving in Hollywood for Christmas 1940. As a foreign doctor he had to requalify in the States, and had arranged to do so by a two-year course in Rochester, New York – thus enforcing a physical separation from Ingrid which was unlikely to do the marriage much good. When *Anna Christie* brought her East to New Jersey, she decided to stay on with Petter and, with no new film even in prospect, to play the housewife instead in upstate New York.

Opposite. Torn between two loves in Casablanca *with Paul Henreid (left) and Humphrey Bogart. Warner Bros.*

This interlude, of nearly a year, served to demonstrate just how far she and Petter had grown apart. What it amounted to was that he still wanted to play the role of the heavy Swedish father, keeping his little girl in order and expecting her to settle to a staid bourgeois life among the other doctors' wives in this relatively small and conservative community. The trouble with that arrangement was that Ingrid had grown out of it. She had been too long away from Petter's protection, making her own life and falling (very selectively) under the influence of other, more colourful 'strong men' like Spencer Tracy and Victor Fleming (the latter reciprocating her feelings with what were eventually to become passionate declarations of love). She did not like playing the placid sweet girl and devoted middle-class wife on screen any more, so why should she like playing the same role in life, where you did not even get to take your makeup off at the end of the day?

She tried manfully, but after two or three months she was going mad from boredom. *For Whom the Bell Tolls* was out of her reach, and to make matters worse Selznick, aware that he had her very much where he wanted her, desperate to come back and work, decided that this was the moment to renegotiate her contract, tying her down to the hated seven years, instead of the year-by-year options she then had – all as a condition of buying for her the current New York hit play *Gaslight* (or *Angel Street* as it was called there). At least her annoyance with this suggestion persuaded her to get herself an agent, which mollified her a bit in her feelings about Selznick, if it did not instantly bring her more work. Finally, however, when she was becoming quite desperate, a project was put to her by Selznick, and though she did not like the idea of the role as described to her very much – another noble woman who got to wear nice clothes – she accepted it just for something to do.

No one in any way involved with *Casablanca* seems to have had the faintest inkling of the mythic status the film was going in retrospect to assume. They were all too busy battling with a non-existent script and trying to understand what they were doing and where they were going day by day. Ingrid, as all the world now knows, was playing a clear-eyed, idealistic heroine, torn between her love for Humphrey Bogart, a hardboiled adventurer with whom she had an affair two years earlier in Paris while believing her husband was dead, and her loyalty to Paul Henreid, the husband in question, and what he stands for in the continuing fight against Nazism. Her complaint about the role and the filming was always, rather naively, that since they did not have an ending for the script until nearly all the film was shot, she did not know whom she would go off with or which of the two she was supposed to love.

It is surprising that the director, Michael Curtiz, did not point out the obvious: that clearly she loves them both in different ways. But then quite possibly he realized, being a very experienced film-maker, that a measure of suspense and uncertainty would give colour and variety to her performance, by preventing her from coming down too plonkingly on one side or the other in the simple either/or choice which was apparently the only way she could comfortably conceive it. Who says, after all, that actors have to be comfortable in order to give of their best? All through her career, Ingrid was very convinced of her ability to see the right way, to interpret all roles in terms of her own reactions, her own sensibility. Too convinced, to the point of complacency, if she did not have a strong (or devious) director to trick her out of a rut and into some new, uncomfortable insights. Certainly, whether by happy accident or deep-laid design, Curtiz, the script and the star chemistry (even though Ingrid felt she never got anywhere near Bogart on a personal level) all worked to extract an interesting performance from her in a role which was not, after all, very interesting, make her look as beautiful as she ever had on screen, and finally propel her, complaining all the way, into

Below. For Whom the Bell Tolls. *Ingrid and Gary Cooper off-set. Paramount.*

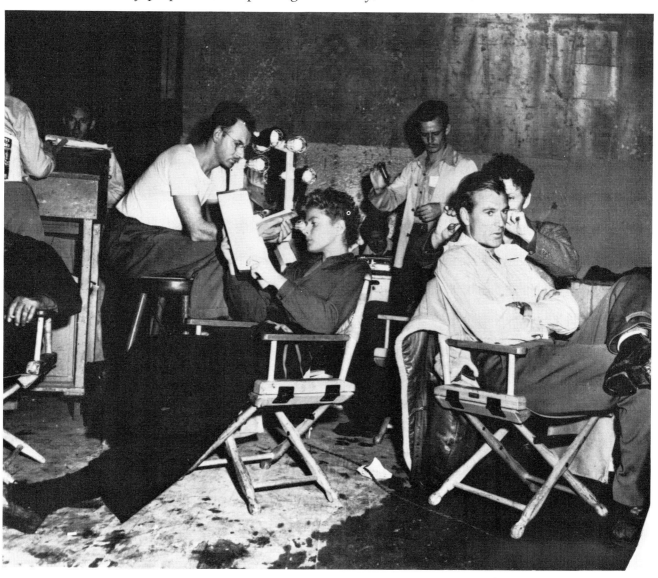

the small elite of top Hollywood stars.

No sooner had she finished shooting *Casablanca* than she got a second chance at *For Whom the Bell Tolls*. Vera Zorina, something of an unknown quantity as a dramatic actress, was not working out, so shooting was stopped while the producers re-cast the vital role of Maria, and this time Ingrid was there, available, and the obvious choice. Obvious, at any rate, by the Hollywood standards of the time (not to mention Hemingway's enthusiastic nomination). In other circumstances one might think this statuesque blonde Swede rather a strange choice for a passionate Spanish peasant. But since this close-knit band of Spanish guerillas also includes, as well as a couple of genuine Latins, the Russians Akim Tamiroff and Vladimir Sokoloff, the Greek Katina Paxinou, and the Italian Eduardo Ciannelli, we should be surprised at nothing.

In any case, this was Hemingway Hollywood-style, with the harsh political realities glossed over and the sex softened almost to the point of non-existence (even the, in its time, notorious

Below. Freedom-fighters, Hollywood-style in For Whom the Bell Tolls. *Paramount.*

scene where Bergman and Cooper share a sleeping-bag could hardly be more innocuous). In her first colour film, Ingrid looks gorgeous, but it cannot truthfully be said that much gritty reality remains: the famous short haircut is so carefully coiffed, the makeup throughout so immaculate, and as she later observed herself, she is allowed to be too obviously happy on screen to get very near the inner conflict of a girl who has been gang-raped and become emotionally frozen until love brings back her will to live. However, it was just the kind of superficially brave, glamorously deglamorized performance that went down well in Hollywood in those days, and won Ingrid her first Oscar nomination, though not yet the award itself. And the film brought her

Opposite. With Gary Cooper in Saratoga Trunk *(a leading man, for once, demonstrably taller). Warner Bros.*

Left. In Saratoga Trunk *as an exotic Creole beauty. Warner Bros.*

into contact with another of the strong men in her life, Gary Cooper, to whom by her own account she reacted like a starry-eyed schoolgirl, gazing at him so adoringly on and off set that her English coach Ruth Roberts had to remonstrate with her. It seems possible that this devotion did not remain so platonic as her other crushes of the decade, but nobody seems to know for sure.

Certainly her relations with her husband, though friendly, were becoming more and more formal and distant. She returned to Rochester and family life, with a brief break making a documentary on *Swedes in America* for the 'Projection of America' series devised by the Office of War Information, in which she lived for a week with a family of Swedish farmers in Minnesota. Immediately after that she went into another film with Gary Cooper – *Saratoga Trunk*, directed like *For Whom the Bell Tolls* by Sam Wood. It was a role she much wanted to play: that of a beautiful Creole (!) adventuress who tangles with a Texas gambler (Gary Cooper) while looking for a rich husband, but realizes in the end (naturally) that he is the one she has loved all along. Being cast against type – much more so than in *For Whom the Bell Tolls* – does wonders for Ingrid's screen image, and the obvious chemistry between her and Cooper also brings an unwonted sparkle to her performance. Oddly, though the film was shot early in 1943, it was not released to American theatres until late 1945 – perhaps because it was felt to be too sophisticated and

Opposite. In Gaslight *with Charles Boyer. MGM.*

Left. Studying the script of Gaslight *in her dressing room with Ruth Roberts. MGM.*

cynical for the taste of home audiences in the darkest days of the war.

Immediately after *Saratoga Trunk* Ingrid got to play another role that she had coveted and thought she had lost. When she refused Selznick's new contract terms for what amounted in her view to a seven-year indenture, he had given up bidding for the rights of *Gaslight*, and the property had been acquired by MGM. Now MGM wanted her to appear in it after all, starring with Charles Boyer as her unscrupulous and finally murderous husband, willing if necessary to drive her insane in order to get his hands on some family jewels. The story called on her to suffer spectacularly (Sardou's old recipe for satisfactory drama, 'Torture the heroine', was very inventively followed in Patrick Hamilton's play) and progress from wide-eyed innocence to bitter worldly wisdom; moreover she would be directed by George Cukor, a film-maker justly renowned for his skill in bringing out the best in actresses. The only fly in the ointment was Selznick, who jibbed at her taking second billing to Charles Boyer. But eventually even he was appeased (enough money would usually do it), and as a reward for being gruellingly put through her dramatic paces, Ingrid actually carried off her first Oscar for the part.

By this time Petter had finished his training in Rochester, and

Above. Ingrid in costume for Gaslight *visits Ronald Colman and Marlene Dietrich in* Kismet *on a neighbouring set. MGM.*

Above. Oscar Ceremony 1944. Ingrid, Barry Fitzgerald (left) and Bing Crosby grasp their awards.

had arranged to do his last year's internship in California, up towards San Francisco but near enough, at least, that he and Ingrid could finally set up house together in Los Angeles. With Ingrid's money they bought a house in Benedict Canyon, and had to settle anew to the business of living together – if they could. In certain things they saw absolutely eye to eye. The matter of money, for instance, where they seem to have carried Swedish frugality to rather absurd extremes: Ingrid never bought new clothes if old ones could be persuaded to do another turn with some slight modification, and they were so determined that Pia should not get any fancy ideas about money that the poor girl seems to have been convinced they were living on the edge of penury – Ingrid once described, in an amused tone, an occasion when Pia had an outburst of hysterical fear because her mother was threatened with a five-dollar ticket for a minor motoring offence. But in other ways their standards were growing farther and farther apart. Petter apparently was feeling a bit of jealousy on his own account at the rumours, inevitable in Hollywood whether well-founded or not, that she was having affairs with her leading men. And she found that his attempts to interfere with the running of her career, though no doubt well-meant, seemed to her often patronizing and ill-judged. So, things were not altogether

good in the Lindstrom/Bergman home, though they remained polite and friendly towards each other and that, Ingrid reflected, was more than many couples they knew had going for them.

In any case, now she was undoubtedly on top of the heap, there was work, work and more work. Selznick kept right on wanting to type-cast her as – in her own words apropros of one offered role – 'a courageous, strong, sincere, good *bore.*' She kept resisting, allegedly in the cause of her art and her desire to expand her acting abilities. If she really thought that, on the whole she was wrong. But if she was in fact actuated by a canny feeling for what sort of role the public would like her in, then she was quite often right. It may be doubted, for instance, if she was really silly enough to think that the sentimental role of the warmhearted impulsive nun with whom Father Bing Crosby tangles in *The Bells of St Mary's* was really a challenge to anyone, least of all herself. But she liked the idea of this unashamed wallow in Hollywood religiosity, noted the enormous success director Leo McCarey had had with its predecessor *Going My Way*, and felt, quite correctly, that with this one slight variation (her dimpling instead of Barry Fitzgerald grumping) the formula could be just as successful a second time. She insisted; Selznick resisted. Or pretended to resist at least until he had got double the normal price for her services (which nearly all went to him, not to her), plus a year's space at RKO Studios free for his own productions, plus the remake rights to three properties owned by RKO (in-

Above. Ailing Ingrid with Father Bing in The Bells of St Mary's. *John Mielhe/RKO.*

Above. Ingrid and Gregory Peck, the audience, watch Hitchcock perform. Selznick-United Artists.

Overleaf. Spellbound: *'Gee, Doctor, you look great without your glasses.' Madison Lacy/Selznick-United Artists.*

cluding *Little Women*, which he wanted for his protegée and wife-to-be Jennifer Jones), at which point he gracefully gave in.

He was, of course, doing very well out of his star, as was his way – though always a film man first and foremost, it was often by a very short head from his interests as a money-man. Since coming to America under contract to him in 1939, Ingrid had made nine feature films and made an average $60,000 a year by 1945. But of those films Selznick had himself produced only the first, *Intermezzo*. For all the rest he had hired her out to other companies, at gradually increasing rates; for *Casablanca*, *For Whom the Bell Tolls* and *Saratoga Trunk* he had charged between $100,000 and $150,000 a picture; *The Bells of St Mary's* represented in money and kind more than $250,000 to him. In return for all this he had produced *Anna Christie* on stage for her (on a very modest scale, be it noted) and had used his influence to get her *For Whom the Bell Tolls*, though not very successfully until Paramount were really desperate. Though Ingrid always maintained that she bore no grudges, feeling it was only fair for him to make something from his confidence in her at a period when, she alleged, no one else had any, her letters from the Forties tell a rather different tale. And it was no doubt at least partially to assuage any lingering resentment that he decided to bring Ingrid and his other great contract name, Alfred Hitchcock, together in a property which he would personally produce.

At this time Hitchcock was in Europe, doing his bit for the war

effort, directing two short films in French for the British government's Central Office of Information. He was in a rather similar position to Ingrid's vis-à-vis Selznick: he had come over in 1939 under contract to Selznick, who had produced his first American film, *Rebecca* – and then nothing except loan-outs which were highly profitable for Selznick but did little for Hitchcock's finances or general peace of mind. However, having been working consistently in Hollywood for five years, he found back in England that he missed the knowhow and the superior technical facilities of the American cinema; possibly he even hankered a little for Selznick himself. When he got back from Britain, he had with him a draft treatment for a psychological thriller eventually to be called *Spellbound*. Selznick was to produce it as his return to filmmaking after five quiescent years, and it was to star two of his contract players, for a change working for him directly: Gregory Peck and Ingrid Bergman.

In after years, Hitchcock would sometimes unkindly murmur: 'Ah, Ingrid. So beautiful, so *stupid* . . .' Psychiatrists such as Ingrid plays in *Spellbound* (if there be any such outside a scriptwriter's frenzied imagination) would no doubt read that as an insecure man's need to desecrate the idol. For certainly in fact Hitchcock and Ingrid hit it off splendidly from the first moment they met, and remained friends right up to his death. He liked her brisk, no-nonsense approach to work; he shared her puritan conscience and her parsimony; and he approved her taste for a good dry martini once the day's work was done. Also, on a rather deeper level, he immediately saw beneath the boring good-girl exterior so prized by Selznick: he appreciated that here was just such a cool Nordic blonde as he had been looking for, one with a fire beneath the surface which could blaze up on screen all the more excitingly because by conventional standards it was so unexpected. If anyone could have guessed at this stage what would happen when Ingrid met Rossellini, it must surely have been Hitchcock.

Professionally Ingrid and Hitchcock were completely in accord. Her role this time round was not all that challenging: she played a glamorous psychiatrist in a clinic who gradually becomes suspicious of the new director (Gregory Peck). He behaves oddly, and eventually reveals that he is suffering from amnesia. But why? And what has happened to the real new director? Has the interloper possibly murdered him? Will he possibly murder Ingrid as well? There is unlikely to be much room for subtle and searching characterization in any story with so many questionmarks. But Ingrid looks beautiful, emotes satisfactorily when torn between love and fear, and definitely leaves her mark on one of Hitchcock's admittedly lesser efforts.

The only real challenge the role seemed likely to offer was one of physical discomfort. Hitchcock wanted the clues in this psychological mystery to be planted in a long dream experienced by the amnesiac hero, and decided that the paintings of the

INGRID
BERGMAN

A magazine cover and film poster depict Ingrid in some of her major roles

Opposite: Joan of Arc. *RKO.*

Below. Anastasia. *20th Century-Fox.*

Top left. With Gary Cooper.
Bottom. With Cary Grant in
Indiscreet. *Warner Bros.*
Opposite top. In A Walk in the
Spring Rain. *Columbia.*
Opposite bottom. In A Matter of
Time. *American International
Pictures.*
Overleaf. A Woman Called Golda.
Paramount Television.

surrealist Salvador Dali, with their hallucinatory clarity and hard, precise finish, conformed most closely to his idea of what dreams were really like. So Dali was brought in to devise the dream sequence. In the event, much more was shot than ended up in the finished film. But on consideration Hitchcock vetoed a detail in a scene where Ingrid was shown as a statue that shattered to reveal her living self inside. Dali wanted her, when the statue broke open, to be covered in ants. And nothing but real ants would be satisfactory. Hitchcock always had a strong sense of the proprieties where stars were concerned, and he definitely did not feel it correct for a star of Ingrid's magnitude to be tangling with thousands of ants, so, much to Ingrid's relief, out this jolly little detail came.

Spellbound turned out, despite its limitations, to be an enormous box-office success: the biggest that either Hitchcock or Ingrid had been associated with so far. Selznick therefore thought it natural to start immediately setting up another film in which Hitchcock would direct and Ingrid star. While this was being arranged and scripted Ingrid decided to do her bit for the war effort (or the just-post-war effort) by going to Europe to entertain the troops in occupied Germany. And in the process, incidentally, she took a further step, though not yet decisive, in the break-up of her semi-detached marriage with Petter. The group of entertainers, which consisted of Ingrid, Jack Benny, Larry Adler and Martha Tilton, arrived in Paris on 6 June 1945, to be greeted by Marlene Dietrich, who was just finishing her tour of duty, with 'Ah, now you're coming, when the war's over.' War or no war, they could hardly have been more warmly welcomed by thousands of home-sick GIs. Ingrid joined Jack Benny in a skit on *Gaslight*, where she was terrorizing him, and gave readings from a new play by Maxwell Anderson which she was planning to do on Broadway, when she would finally be fulfilling her lifelong ambition to play St Joan.

The tour was gruelling but satisfying. More important to Ingrid personally, though, and to her image of herself and her own possibilities, was her meeting in Paris with the famous war photographer Robert Capa. She had only just arrived when she got a funny note from Capa and Irwin Shaw, neither of whom she had met or, she claims, heard of, offering her the choice of flowers or dinner, since they could not afford both. She accepted the dinner, and immediately hit it off in a very special way with Capa. A way which led very rapidly to a passionate affair – the first extra-marital relationship she specifically admitted to. And, quite likely, the first there ever was. For Ingrid was, in this as in most other things, still very strict, very Swedish, very puritanical. Her relationship with Petter had got more and more distant through the American years, but such as it was it seems to have provided her with adequate protection from the realization of her own passionate, over-emotional nature. The hero-worshipping crushes on strong, older men seem really to have been enough, providing a necessary emotional outlet without going far enough actually to challenge her deepest moral assumptions. (There is a curious parallel here with Hitchcock, in his strongly emotional but technically non-sexual relationships with his succession of cool blonde stars: when he claimed that Ingrid fell in love with him he was no doubt right, though one would say it must have been to exactly the same extent and within exactly the same limits as he fell in love with her.)

Capa, though, was something different. For one thing, he was possibly the first strong man she had met who was eager to take the relationship a stage or two further than loving friendship, and was (in her eyes) free to do so, being unmarried. But what about her? Was she free? Though still married, she could hardly feel any more a binding sense of duty to Petter. She was far from home and, even though the war in Europe was over, in a world where psychological priorities were very different from the secure lotus-land of Los Angeles. The feeling of living on the brink was still strong, especially with someone like Capa, who seemed somehow to need danger as a sort of drug: he was one of those people who become fully themselves only in war, and have the sensation of only half-living in peacetime. Obviously the sense of danger which clung to him was part of the attraction, and the sense, too, that he was doomed – there could be only so many more chances before his luck ran out.

All the same, Ingrid would certainly have asked Petter for a divorce and married Capa if he had not made it clear from the outset that marrying and settling down was not and never had been part of his calculations. 'Legitimizing' the promptings of her nature in this way was still important to Ingrid. And indeed, much of the trouble which was to come to her in her relationship with Rossellini would never have happened to someone more devious, less strictly moral in her upbringing and present responses. As it was, the Capa affair could be only a brief interlude – though Ingrid remained friendly with him and in regular touch until his death nine years later, in Indo-China chasing another war – but it played a crucial role in breaking down her conventional attitudes and showing her that life had other possibilities for her beyond satisfying her passionate need for work, work and more work.

But that, for the moment, remained the answer. Back in Hollywood, she went straight into the new Hitchcock film, *Notorious*. Selznick had prepared it, with almost the same team as *Spellbound*: Hitchcock directing, Ben Hecht writing, and Ingrid starring, though this time with Cary Grant. Then, in one of his spectacular, unaccountable bits of wheeler-dealing, he had sold off the whole thing as a package to RKO for $800,000 and half the profits. So Hitchcock was in the happy position of producing for himself, doing just what he liked, without Selznick looking – as he was increasingly inclined to do – over his director's and writer's shoulder and constantly interfering. In consequence the

Opposite. In Notorious *with her favourite leading man, Cary Grant. RKO.*

shooting went remarkably smoothly and quickly, though Ingrid, by her own admission, had moments of vagueness when she just could not get into the scene. But Hitchcock was very patient with her, and the result was one of her best performances, in a role which conformed with her deeper nature rather than having her typecast according to the well-scrubbed stereotype.

Ingrid plays a passionate woman who has gone to pieces (in a tactfully unspecified fashion) after her father was convicted as a German spy. She is recruited for counter-espionage by Cary Grant, but before she can begin they fall in love. The rest of the film is based on the unspoken conflict between two proud, uptight natures. When she has to insinuate herself into the affections of a leading Nazi in Brazil (Claude Rains), and eventually to marry him, she waits for her boss to tell her not to, to renounce her job for love of him, while he waits for her to break and refuse to go through with the scheme. Hence a lot of agonizing on both sides before it becomes clear that her husband has realized she is playing a double game and is gradually poisoning her, and at the last possible moment she is rescued. Just this sort of conflict between the dictates of passion and of duty was right at the

Opposite. Portrait in costume from Notorious. *RKO.*

Left. Ingrid at the time of the filming of Notorious. *E. Bachrach/RKO.*

centre of Ingrid's nature, especially after her recent affair with Capa, and so she could identify completely with the role, while her love scenes with Cary Grant had a new intensity, sufficient to get the Johnson office all hot and bothered, though Hitch had cunningly shot the long kissing scene in such a way that, while there was no doubt about the spirit of the thing, it scrupulously obeyed the letter of Production Code law about how long a single kiss could last.

Notorious marked, as it happened, the end of Ingrid's long association with Selznick: it filled out the sixth of the yearly options following her first year under contract to him and enough was enough. Also Petter, a little put out by the small part he could play in her professional career, felt that at least he could aid her in money matters, and insisted that once she could be free of Selznick and make her own decisions, she must do so. Selznick, of course, insisted on seeing her refusal to sign up again with him as a personal betrayal, and for a while would not even speak to her. This upset her, because in spite of everything she continued to look upon him as 'my father, my guide and leader.' They did formally make it up before she left Hollywood late in 1946 to do *Joan of Lorraine* on Broadway, and eventually became good friends again – though that did not prevent him from announcing, as the play was about to open, that he was going to produce a Joan of Arc film with – of course – Jennifer Jones in the lead. (Ingrid's matter-of-fact comment on that was, 'Good: then we can hire you our costumes.')

Curiously enough, many stars and directors who have chafed under the Hollywood contract system, and been loud in their determination to take their own career decisions once they got the chance, have proved in the event adept at making all the wrong decisions. Ingrid, unfortunately, was to be no exception to the rule. Left to herself, she would never have made *Casablanca*, the film that made her a superstar. She was not eager, at the outset, to work with Hitchcock: the prospect of making *The Bells of St Mary's* for Leo McCarey excited her much more. That, at least, whatever aesthetic limitations the film might have, was a sensible choice in terms of the public and building her popularity. But for the first two independent productions she managed to pick films which had neither high aesthetic qualities nor broad popular appeal: by the time she landed up in Italy to make *Stromboli* she was coming close to being regarded as box office poison, and she really had no one to blame but herself.

In point of fact, she always subsequently maintained that she was talked into the first, *Arch of Triumph,* against her better judgement. She never felt right about the character she was to play, a loose-living nightclub singer who has an overshadowed affair with a doctor (Charles Boyer) who saves her from suicide at the beginning and shoots her in a fit of jealousy at the end. She doubted whether she could believe in the character or make her believable to others. But she had had such doubts before, and

Opposite. Arch of Triumph.
Enterprise-United Artists.

everything had worked out all right. And this time the chemistry seemed right: she was co-starred again with Charles Boyer, with whom she had previously had considerable success in *Gaslight*, and the director, Lewis Milestone, was working again on a novel by Erich Maria Remarque, with whom he had previously had his biggest success, *All Quiet on the Western Front*. With Charles Laughton also starring (as a sadistic Nazi) and an emigré German playwright called Bertolt Brecht writing additional dialogue, what could go wrong?

In the event, practically everything. The film came out much over-length, and in the cutting lost most of whatever coherence it originally had. It ended up long, heavy and flat, with much too little incident to carry the rather sodden love story. When it eventually opened, almost eighteen months later, no one liked it, and though Ingrid got the usual nod from the critics for her beauty and authority, she was proved quite right in her initial doubts: no one believed in her as a shakily reformed trollop who quite heartlessly keeps two men dangling at the same time. The film was the first production of a new company called Enterprise

Right. Ingrid being directed by Lewis Milestone in Arch of Triumph.
Enterprise-United Artists.

73

Studios, which was vowed to making superior, artistic films on a profit-sharing basis. Since there were no profits from *Arch of Triumph* all these lofty ambitions came to nothing; but Ingrid did not have too much time left to worry about that. During the shooting Robert Capa turned up in Hollywood, and they recognized both that they were in love and that they would never get married. And as soon as shooting was finished, Ingrid had to set off eastwards, towards Broadway.

There, on the other side of the country, Maxwell Anderson's *Joan of Lorraine* had been slowly coming together. It was not just a simple matter of Ingrid's reading a play script, liking it and doing it. Perhaps Anderson was not enough of a strong man for her, or perhaps she was not really so much in awe of strong men as she always pretended. But anyway, while she loved the idea of playing St Joan she was not satisfied at the outset that this was the right play. Anderson's idea was to make a modern drama about the mental conflicts of an actress playing St Joan, with key scenes from St Joan's life given in rehearsal form as a play within a play. Ingrid felt there was too much about the actress and too little about Joan, and so gradually, in the months that the project was under discussion, she worked Anderson more and more round to her way of thinking, toughening up his rather sentimental conception of Joan with materials she had found in the transcripts of the original trial and the unvarnished reports of eye-witnesses.

She was still not wholly satisfied with the text when the play opened in November 1945, and was to get another stab at it when the play was adapted to the screen two years later. Whatever her reservations, the play production went down very well, the New York critics were ecstatic about her, and she won the Antoinette Perry Award for that year. One critic in particular, Louis Kronenberger, put his finger on her true, unique quality when he observed: 'She is radiant and enchanting – perhaps not as an actress but simply as a human being.' In other words, even when quite palpably acting, she remained the star first and foremost – it was her personality shining through the role which captured audiences' attention and provoked a peculiarly personal kind of affection. After all, anyone can, with a bit of training, 'act', but this particular kind of personal charisma is vouchsafed to very few: the ability to fascinate, not by doing something, but just by existing on stage or in front of a camera.

As it happened, the stage success of *Joan of Lorraine* was to give her immediately another opportunity to play St Joan, this time in front of a camera: it finally convinced Hollywood, or at least enough of Hollywood, that her instinct had been right all the time, that this was the role she was born to play. One evening after the show Victor Fleming, whom she had hardly seen since working with him on *Doctor Jekyll and Mr Hyde*, came bursting into her dressing-room insisting that she must make the film immediately, and, moreover, putting up a concrete proposal which involved the combination of Fleming, Ingrid and producer

Walter Wanger into a production company called Sierra Pictures, so that they would have complete control over what they were doing.

As far as Ingrid was concerned, that meant bringing the character of Joan nearer to her own concept of it, trying to catch the reality of the simple French peasant girl, as indicated in the contemporary documents, whereas Anderson had turned her into a very sweet, feminine character perfectly suited to the illustration of his own philosophical points but having very little, even after Ingrid's suggestions, to do with the historical reality. Anderson, unfortunately, was writing the screenplay for the film, and though he agreed to drop the modern framework and make the script completely into a history of Joan's life, he still clung stubbornly to his original conception of the character. After a while the partners decided, regretfully, to fire him and bring in another writer. When the stage run of *Joan of Lorraine* was concluded Ingrid headed straight back to Hollywood, 'back into the cage, (to) sit in the sun, obey Petter and be sober and look eighteen years old,' as she put it at the time in a letter to Ruth Roberts.

On the film front, there was an endless struggle by the independents to raise money to go into production; there were the

Right. In Joan of Lorraine *on the New York stage with the play's director, Sam Wanamaker.*

manifold problems with the script; and there was the slight complication that Victor Fleming had fallen hopelessly in love with Ingrid. When they were apart he wrote her passionate love-letters; when they were together they hardly had time to consider the question, with so much work to do on the film. And in Hollywood they were both in the bosom of their respective families, which all added to the intense guilt-feelings Fleming had at being involved like this with a woman half his age. One would suppose that all this banked-up emotion would in some way affect the film, even if Ingrid's lengthy quest for the truth about St Joan did not. But, saddeningly, all the fuss and bother went for nothing: *Joan of Arc* comes no nearer to genuine religious feeling than *The Bells of St Mary's*. It is big, glossy, studio-bound and very solemn, over-concerned with its 'important' story and keeping up a lofty tone. Ingrid looks beautiful, remains relatively unsmudged by every battle, and plays throughout with a fervent gaze which has more to do with the Hollywood stereotype of saintliness than with history or true feeling. Again, the great chance had somehow eluded her. What a pity she did not do Shaw's *Saint Joan* instead: but when, the following year, she actually met the sage of Ayot St Lawrence she told him in no uncertain terms that she did not like his version because he made Joan too clever. In the film, a little more cleverness all round would not have come amiss.

It was around the time Ingrid was making *Joan of Arc* that she and Petter made what was to prove a fateful visit to an art cinema on La Cienega in West Hollywood. It was to see what all the fuss was about with this much-touted Italian neo-realism, the films shot with largely non-professional actors on the streets where their stories had really happened. The first example of it to arrive locally was Roberto Rossellini's *Rome – Open City*, made in the most primitive conditions in the streets of Rome during the last days of the war. Used – all too used – to Hollywood gloss and production values, the whole studio system of factory production, Ingrid was completely bowled over by this new way of cinema, and at once, impulsively, announced that she must find out more; the man who could make such a film must be a marvel. A few months later she was in New York doing a radio show and went to see another Rossellini film, *Paisan*, in a small art cinema on Broadway. This confirmed her first feeling: now she felt she must write to Rossellini and see if by any chance she could make a film with him.

So she wrote the famous 'Ti amo' letter:

> I saw your films *Open City* and *Paisan* and enjoyed them very much. If you need a Swedish actress who speaks English very well, who has not forgotten her German, who is not very understandable in French and who in Italian knows only 'Ti amo', I am ready to come and make a film with you. Best regards, Ingrid Bergman.

Opposite. Joan of Arc *on screen.* RKO.

Though it later emerged that when Rossellini got the letter, by a very roundabout route, he claimed to have no idea who Ingrid Bergman was and finally managed to place her only from having seen the original Swedish version of *Intermezzo* in an air-raid — he wrote back enthusiastically, lying smoothly: 'It is absolutely true that I dreamed of making a film with you,' and announcing that now he was inspired to look for possible subjects. This was satisfactory, if not very conclusive, and there matters might have stood, if Ingrid had not been due at that moment to go to Europe, where Hitchcock was preparing to shoot their third picture together, *Under Capricorn*, in a British studio.

In various ways this moment seemed like an end and a beginning. Though relations remained correct between her and Petter, and the question of a divorce, first raised in 1945 (because, Ingrid alleged, Petter announced quite seriously in the middle of one of their arguments that he never made mistakes, and she thought, 'I cannot live with a person who believes that he doesn't make mistakes'), had been shelved by mutual consent, the failure of *Arch of Triumph* and *Joan of Arc* had shaken Ingrid's faith in Petter's business sense, the one area where she always deferred to him. During *Arch of Triumph* she and Capa had agreed that their romance was going nowhere, and during the shooting of *Under Capricorn* they decided to part for good (though not before Petter had become awkwardly jealous at the obvious strength of feeling between them). And then Ingrid's latest 'strong man', Victor Fleming, had died of a heart attack just a few weeks after the opening of *Joan of Arc*. If all these doors were closing, it was inevitable that Ingrid should be unconsciously ready for another door to open.

ITALY

Possibly, as Hitchcock thought, rationalizing after the event, Ingrid's sense of aimlessness and restlessness at this time harmed her work on *Under Capricorn*. But even without that danger, it would not have been a very promising prospect for either of them. Ingrid would inevitably have difficulty being accepted as English – something very different in audience's minds from playing assorted French and Spaniards. Hitchcock himself seemed to be going through a period of middle-aged uncertainty such as afflicts many successful men in their late forties. If he could not be blamed for the heaviness and lifelessness of *The Paradine Case*, the last film he made before finally freeing himself of his contractual obligations to Selznick (Selznick forced quite unsuitable casting on him and interfered with every aspect of the production), the fact remains that there is an aridity and an apparent preoccupation with technical devices over the demands of the story which mars a whole group of the films he made after *Notorious*.

In *Under Capricorn* he had planned to use extensively, if not continuously, the device of the 'ten-minute take' he had developed in *Rope*, which virtually eliminated editing. Those around him felt that this made an already heavy and old-fashioned subject (a period piece set in Australia about a woman with a dark secret which has driven her to drink and spread misery and intrigue all around her) even slower and more ponderous. In any case, his actors were petrified by it, because one fluffed line or one technical flaw of some kind could wreck a whole day's preparation and shooting. Eventually, Hitchcock agreed to modify his chosen style slightly, mainly for technical reasons, and from then on the shooting went more smoothly. But the script was still heavy and talkative, and the atmosphere on the film was not at all happy. On one occasion there happened what Hitchcock always feared most: a confrontation. Unnerved by being followed round endlessly by his wretched travelling camera, Ingrid proceeded to tell him on set just how much she hated the new technique, while the rest of the cast and crew sat round in an embarrassed silence. Hitchcock made no answer; just went home for the rest of the day and continued in the morning as though nothing had happened.

The one gleam of light in all this was that something seemed finally to be happening with the Rossellini idea. In London Ingrid received a letter explaining that he now had a subject, called *Terra di Dio*. That was all. Despite her sincere eagerness to be part of this new European cinema, Ingrid had been in Hollywood too long to be content with so little. What was the plot, where was the script, how long was the shooting schedule, what language would the film be shot in? Should they not, above all, get together to talk about it? Rossellini wrote back agreeing. He was just off to Amalfi to shoot some film, but why did they not arrange to meet in Paris at the Georges V whenever it would fit in with her filming on *Under Capricorn*? She telegraphed back suggesting a date when she and Petter, who was with her in

Opposite. Under Capricorn: 'Torture the heroine.' Warner Bros.

England, could come over for a weekend to talk. She little realized the explosion that would be caused by the arrival of her telegram in Amalfi. At this time, Rossellini was living with Anna Magnani, the star of *Open City*, and when she saw him receive the telegram with an air of secrecy she decided to dump a whole plate of spaghetti over him in public. *Terra di Dio* had first been designed for her, and whether the spaghetti incident derived from a woman's intuition working overtime or happened because she had some inkling of this professional slight no one could say for sure.

However, it is amazing how frequently the existence of jealousy creates an occasion for it. Faceful of spaghetti notwithstanding, Rossellini was in Paris at the suggested time, and from the first moment Ingrid was aware of a powerful magnetism. Rossellini was not conventionally handsome, no taller than Ingrid, and about ten years older. But when he talked his eyes flashed; he seemed so intelligent and original; and he knew just who he was, what he was doing and where he was going. Almost an identikit portrait of Ingrid's strong man type, in fact. (And also, almost a Hitchcock with sex appeal.) Whether he felt anything special at this first meeting is not recorded. But since he felt strongly enough about the possibilities of the situation to make over for Ingrid a story he had first discussed with Anna Magnani (and weather the volcanic consequences), he may well have fantasized some possibilities, even while carefully playing everything by ear. At this meeting they got no further than agreeing that they were both eager to work together on the project (so much so on her part that when Petter started to raise difficulties over the nicer points of personal expenses Ingrid told him in Swedish to cool it), and that Rossellini would send her a plot outline as soon as possible. As for the rest, he just did not know. He was used to scripting as he went along, shooting films in five or six weeks (which by Hollywood standards was an incredibly short time), and taking little or no notice of what words his actors said, in what language, because it would all be dubbed afterwards anyway.

To Ingrid it all sounded alarming but good. She and Petter went off to London to finish *Under Capricorn* and await further developments. In November 1948, back in Hollywood, Ingrid received the promised synopsis. In the New Year of 1949 Rossellini won the New York Critics Award for *Open City*, and after collecting it came on over to Hollywood to stay with the Lindstroms. While he was there Ingrid made an attempt to interest Goldwyn in backing the film, but after a disastrous showing of Rossellini's gloomy *Germany, Year Zero* at one of Goldwyn's dinner parties that notion fell by the wayside. Then, out of the blue, Howard Hughes got in touch, wanting to get Ingrid under contract to RKO, of which he had recently acquired complete control. There was a history of aggressive flirtation on his part and polite put-down on hers going back a year or two, so she would hardly have contacted him off her own bat. But since the offer was there, it

Above. Rossellini welcomes Ingrid to Italy.

seemed silly not to take it up. Hughes made no secret of regarding *Terra di Dio* (or *Stromboli* as it was soon to be retitled) as a necessary folly for her, a little bit of fun before they got started with the business of seriously making movies. Whatever his attitude, though, he was backing the movie, and plans could go ahead. On 11 March Ingrid left Los Angeles for New York, and by 20 March she had arrived in Rome.

What then happened, though no doubt factual in outline, has come through the years to belong more and more to the realm of movie fantasy. Especially as the circumstances in which the Bergman/Rossellini romance came about grow ever more remote and inconceivable. Even at the time, the fact that it happened at all was not so extraordinary: as Ingrid noted rather bitterly in a letter to Petter four months later, during that time Paulette Goddard had got divorced, Ann Todd had got divorced and married her new director, David Lean, and Viveca Lindfors, Ginger Rogers, Joan Fontaine and Alida Valli were all suing for divorce with no one making a tremendous fuss about it. (She might have added that Rita Hayworth's romance with Ali Khan was also hitting the headlines.) Divorces were, after all, not exactly unknown in Hollywood, whatever hypocritical standards were paid lip-service by the Louella Parsonses and the Hedda Hoppers. Why me, Ingrid undoubtedly thought; why *me*?

For the answer to that we must look to the special qualities which made her and kept her a star. And, of course, to the naivety of the American fan. To an extent Selznick and Michael Curtiz, urging her to accept type-casting and play only the sort of role the public would expect of her, were correct. Not that she should deliberately do it; but because it was bound to happen in the public mind whatever she did to counter it. Her type was unmistakably that of the 'good woman', the natural, healthy, unspoilt person who did not bother with makeup, did not care what she wore, but always looked ravishing anyway. Of course the recent association with nuns and saints did not help either: the public was notoriously incapable of distinguishing the singer from the song, and it was not so long since Jennifer Jones's divorce, entirely unscandalous as it was, had caused tidal waves of misplaced sentiment and outrage, only because on screen she had just played Saint Bernadette. Did anyone seriously expect any actress who played a saint to be a saint in private life? Yes, absolutely.

In addition, there was this very special, personal relationship Bergman fans seemed to feel they had with their loved one. When, at the height of the frenzy a year later, Senator Edwin C. Johnson of Colorado launched his astonishing attack on Ingrid on the floor of the Senate, the tone is unmistakably one of personal betrayal: 'She was a sweet and understanding person,' he wailed, 'with an attractive personality which captivated everyone on and off the screen.' Again and again the same tone recurs: how could she do this to us? – as though all the men of America were married to her and all the women of America somehow tarnished by her 'moral turpitude'.

But what actually happened? Nothing very astonishing, or even very unusual. Finding little or no satisfaction in the dying embers of a twelve-year-old marriage – one in which divorce had been discussed already more than once – Ingrid fell under the spell of a dynamic, unpredictable, brilliant man who happened also to be her director and therefore doubly the father-figure she had always craved. Of course she fell in love with him; of course, almost as inevitably, he fell in love with her. Since she was an almost painfully conventional lady, she could hardly see the situation in terms other than that she must get divorced from her husband and marry Rossellini instead. Naturally she was not schooled in deviousness, had no idea how to hide her emotions or think before she spoke. Even without the constant attentions of the Italian paparazzi buzzing round like flies and building up the 'love-rivalry' between her and Anna Magnani, she would not have been notably well-equipped to handle the situation in the most tactful way possible. And what she actually did, as Petter delayed over the divorce, was to become pregnant by Rossellini. In those days, people did not do things like that – or only in the deadliest secret, on an extended trip to Mexico for their health.

At this distance of time, with all the film stars who have refused to marry the fathers of their children since, who cares? After all, Ingrid did marry Rossellini as soon as she was legally able, and went on to have twins by him, in wedlock, during the five years covered by their tempestuous relationship. They also contrived to make five feature films together, as well as collaborating on a major stage production that toured Europe. Even though opinions have differed, and continue to do so, about the value of their collaborative efforts, it can hardly be said that all the trouble had no tangible results: many bigger storms have resulted in less.

But all this is to anticipate. The arrival in Rome was, like all good Italian scandals, a lot of smoke with, for the moment, precious little fire. Almost as though something akin to national honour was at stake, the Italian press wanted, needed this Italian

Right. The Romance is under way.

intellectual hero to conquer the proud Nordic beauty. It had to be love, or what was the point of it? From the first day, any hotel in which Ingrid stayed was in a state of siege. For a week Rossellini showed her Rome, and they were followed everywhere by crowds. Then they headed south, to Capri, and the photographers went with them, every hour of the day and, if possible, the night. Finally a picture appeared in *Life* magazine of them climbing some steps on the Amalfi coast, together, hand-in-hand. Well, of course American moviegoers, used to decoding what film-makers could sneak past the Production Code, knew perfectly well that that could mean only *one thing*. The scandal was now of international proportions, before it had even really started.

Somehow, they got started with the filming. In many more or less predictable ways they were interrupted: bad weather, indecision over casting, the ubiquitous press photographers, Rossellini's method of improvising as the mood took him and then sorting everything out afterwards. Ingrid had her first shock when Rossellini picked up two burly young fishermen along the way and said casually that one of them would be her leading man – she could choose when they got to Stromboli. She did not at first believe him, but soon found that this was literal fact: they tried first the more likely-looking, tall and handsome, but then decided that the shorter one came over better on screen, so he got the role instead. (All he wanted to know about the job was, when did he get to kiss the girl?) Ingrid was playing a Czech (originally a Latvian) DP who marries an Italian soldier to get out of the internment camp, and then when he is demobilized goes back with him to his island, Stromboli, where he is a simple fisherman. Since that is about all the story there is – the rest is a mood piece about her difficulties fitting in with the community and getting to know her husband – she was not likely to be any wiser at the end of shooting than she was at the beginning. But that, as Rossellini told her from the start, that was the point of the exercise. It was a joint exploration of this woman's psyche, and if they knew exactly what story they were setting out to tell before they started, why should they bother to make the film?

That was all very well, but it was rather like walking a high wire without a safety net. At least with the traditional Hollywood methods Ingrid was used to, you knew in advance if you had a film, though obviously that did not guarantee it would be a good one. By Rossellini's method you might work and explore and shoot, and at the end of the day it would never come together into a satisfactory whole. Even such a failure could be humanly significant and worthwhile, but it was difficult to reconcile with the requirements of film-making as a business. And to avoid at least the occasional disaster, you had to be a genius all the time; craftsmanship was not enough. Even Rossellini, though he consistently behaved like a genius, could not always live up to this in practice.

There was an argument then, and there has been argument ever

Opposite. Stromboli: *shooting on the brink of the volcano. RKO.*

since, about whether he did so in *Stromboli*. If he did not, it was easy enough to make excuses: there was front-office pressure from Hollywood, and eventually the threat to cut off funds and abandon the picture altogether if he ran any further over schedule (by then his 'five or six weeks' had stretched to more than three months). Meanwhile Ingrid, at just the time she needed the most peace and concentration to acclimatize herself to this new, more demanding way of making films, was under mounting pressure, from RKO, from Joseph Breen of the Production Code Office, and from old friends and recent colleagues such as Walter Wanger, to abandon her romance with Rossellini, or at least deny it very firmly and be much more circumspect in the future. The fate not only of *Stromboli*, but also of *Joan of Arc*, currently on release in America, and *Under Capricorn*, due out that autumn, was unequivocally said to be in her hands. Nor was the need to account, if she could, for her behaviour to Petter and Pia, now ten years old, any less personally disturbing. And then, once *Stromboli* was finished and delivered, RKO completely recut it, over the protests of Rossellini, who claimed that in the process whatever narrative sense and atmospheric qualities it had originally possessed were totally lost.

In the circumstances, it would be a miracle if *Stromboli* were the hoped-for masterpiece, and even its greatest admirers seldom claim that the miracle happened. Ingrid seems to be ill at ease throughout, called upon to function not really as a star, Hollywood style, but not really as an actress either. What is going on in her character's mind remains a mystery – and not, unfortunately, a very interesting mystery. There are scenes that have a certain slow, brooding intensity, but it is essentially a very quiet, played-down, interior film which, even had it been far better

Opposite and below. Ingrid in Stromboli. *RKO.*

done, could hardly have met all the irrelevant and rather prurient expectations of the public at large – such of them, that is, as were not so shocked by the publicity that they were staying away in droves. But at least both Rossellini and Ingrid must be given full credit for trying, in very difficult conditions, to follow out their original vision without compromise: *Stromboli* is, at the very least, an extraordinary film for any top Hollywood star at that time to even dream of making – whether or not she was in love with the director.

A major irony in the situation was that Ingrid was the last person in the world to be comfortable in the role of a scarlet woman. She was deeply depressed and racked with guilt, feeling that she had let everybody down. Lines of communication between Stromboli and Hollywood being what they were, a lot of unnecessary ill-will was built up because people who should have been told personally this or that were likely to hear first when they read it in the papers. On 5 August 1949, Ingrid bowed to pressure sufficiently to announce she was starting divorce proceedings at once. The next day a Rome newspaper announced, unofficially of course but correctly, that she was pregnant. This brought Hedda Hopper over on the next plane; Ingrid saw her and was able to gain a little time by equivocating. But the pregnancy made her divorce and Rossellini's that much more urgent. And Petter, seldom the most amenable of men, was in no mood to hurry. Negotiations dragged on through to many intermediaries, including some who were not too wisely chosen, such as an American lawyer in Rome who went back to America for Ingrid and immediately started throwing sensational press-conferences and having intimate documents about her marriage to Petter published in the yellow press. That definitely did not help matters. And the rumour of the baby, once started, could not be long laid to rest: Howard Hughes was told, in the strictest confidence, and decided the best thing for the film was to garner maximum publicity of any kind (when it eventually opened in America it was sold like a repeat of his great scandal-success *The Outlaw*), so he gave the story to the Los Angeles papers, and it was inescapably public property.

Hedda, having been cheated of a scoop, was not pleased. Louella ransacked world history to support her initial assertion that 'Few women in history, or men either, have made the sacrifice the Swedish star has made for love.' All the self-appointed protectors of public morality in the States were up in arms. And back in Italy the siege Ingrid was living under did nothing but intensify, to reach a bizarre and farcical climax in and around the nursing home where Ingrid's son Robertino was born on 2 February 1950. The photographers employed every conceivable ruse to get the first pictures of mother and child, climbing up the drainpipes, dressing up as doctors and nurses, begging to be allowed to dispel rumours that Ingrid had given birth to a monster. . . . One Italian paper even published what appeared to be a family group with Ingrid, the child and Rossellini, the proud father, gazing down on them from the bedside. Only if you looked very carefully could you discover that this was in fact a photomontage . . .

The frenzy reached its climax with Senator Johnson's speech in the US Senate on 14 March, which concluded grandly: 'If out of the degradation associated with *Stromboli*, decency and common-sense can be established in Hollywood, Ingrid Bergman will not have destroyed her career for naught. Out of her ashes may come a better Hollywood.' But inevitably things were going to quieten down a bit, as people of reasonably good will everywhere began to feel that, whatever one's moral standards, this was an absurd amount of fuss to make about one child born out of wedlock. In Rome, Ingrid and Rossellini had more fiddly, practical issues to contend with. He was finishing work on another film, based on the *Little Flowers of St Francis*, and had managed to get his Italian marriage annulled. She was still struggling with the complications of being a Swedish citizen in Italy trying to divorce an uncooperative American citizen in Los Angeles. The only way not readily open to contest was a Mexican divorce, and this came through on 9 February, too late for Robertino's birth certificate: if Ingrid had been listed on it as his mother while she was still legally married to Petter, Petter would legally have been the father, so Robertino had to be listed instead as the son of Rossellini and an undisclosed mother.

Then there was the little matter of how and where Ingrid and Rossellini could get married, given that neither Sweden or the States recognized a proxy Mexican divorce, while Italy would not permit a civil ceremony without documentary evidence that Ingrid had a valid divorce in her country of origin. So, after a Mexican proxy divorce it had to be a Mexican proxy wedding: not a very satisfactory solution, but the best that could be done in the circumstances, and at least it made Ingrid feel like an honest women again, if only on a flimsy technicality. And anyway, it did provide a formula by which she and Rossellini could gradually slip out of the limelight and become more or less private citizens as yesterday's headlines faded from memory. Moreover, she kept insisting on her decision to give up acting after *Stromboli*, to dwindle into a wife and mother, and the disastrous box-office record of her last four films in a row made it look rather as though she might have no choice in the matter.

Petter, understandably resentful, not only because Ingrid had left him, but also because the circumstances had shattered the privacy he had always absolutely insisted on for himself and Pia on the margins of Ingrid's film star life, and cheated him of an important position in neurosurgery as those responsible baulked at the scandalous association, was not being any too helpful in resolving Ingrid's main worry at the time: her relations with Pia. It is hard, looking back, not to feel that in this context Ingrid and Petter acted as two proud, self-centred people who too readily permitted the child to become a pawn in the elaborate game that

91

Above. Peter and Pia set off for Europe to see Ingrid.

was going on between them. On the other hand, it is difficult to see how they could have managed things much better: such delicate matters are not easily decided in a constant glare of publicity. What is certain is that for some years Pia felt, quite understandably, let down and abandoned by her mother, and Ingrid's refusal to see her on her first visit to America after *Stromboli*, in 1957, only reopened old wounds. (Ingrid claimed that she feared she would get too emotional; Pia suspected that, as so often, what Ingrid mainly cared about was her career and her own well-being – perhaps the vision of motherhood in *Autumn Sonata* is not so far off the mark after all.)

Anyway, life was in no way simple for Ingrid those first years in Italy. Endless legal wrangles, extreme professional problems, a strange country and a strange language to get used to, and Rossellini, who, though she loved him and continued to believe with single-minded passion in his genius, was an impossible person, given to throwing tantrums about anything or nothing and behaving like a spoilt child if ever he was called upon to do anything that, at the moment, he did not feel like doing. After the nightmarish experience of *Stromboli*, Ingrid was not even totally convinced that they worked well together: it was quite possible that, whatever the personal attraction, professionally they might be mutually destructive. However, she chafed, as always, at inactivity, and it was becoming painfully obvious that Rossellini's best way to raise finance for a new film was to capitalize on his

still famous wife. In autumn 1951 they went back to work together on *Europa 51*, another study of an emotionally displaced person: Ingrid and Alexander Knox are prosperous Americans living in Rome whose young son kills himself because he feels neglected, and in consequence Ingrid, driven by guilt, indulges in all sorts of undirected acts of philanthropy which start as mild eccentricity and end in madness.

This film was not shown in the States for three years, and was not well received anywhere: the few critics who bothered to consider it seriously tended to feel that such an intense, interior story needed more precise, disciplined treatment than Rossellini, with his improvisatory, hit-or-miss methods of filming, could give it. As with all the films Ingrid made with Rossellini, there have been attempts since to discover *Europa 51* as an unrecognized masterpiece, but they do not altogether carry conviction: it is usually easier to respect the attempt than the achievement, and give higher marks for good intentions than for results.

By the time *Europa 51* was finished, Ingrid was pregnant again, and in 1952 she gave birth to twin girls, Isabella and Ingrid. The event was attended with no great amount of publicity, and that summer Ingrid and Rossellini were able to make a little film which is hardly more than a home movie, just for fun: it was an episode in *Siamo Donne*, which purported to give some behind-the-scenes insight into the lives and personalities of six actresses (including also Ingrid's old arch-enemy Anna Magnani), and

Images from Europa '51
(The Greatest Love). *IFE.*

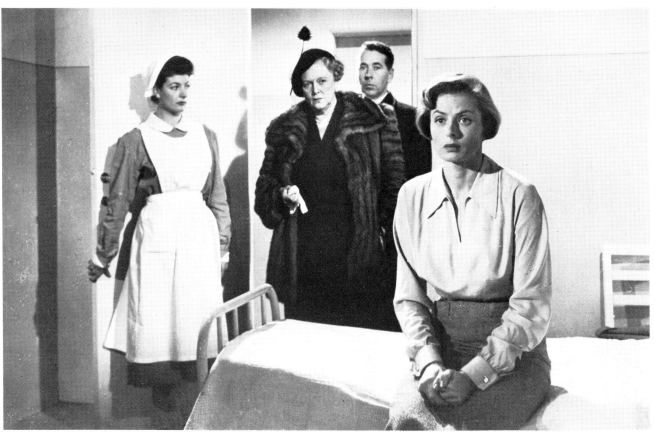

showed Ingrid in very lighthearted mood engaged in a war to the death with a neighbouring chicken who is determined to eat all the prize roses from her garden. This apart, Ingrid was off the screen until 1954, when Rossellini devised another vehicle for her, *Viaggio in Italia* (sometimes called *Strangers* in English), about a bored married couple (Ingrid and George Sanders) whose inheritance of a house in Italy, when they are on the brink of divorce, somehow mysteriously brings them together and heartens them to try again. By this time, of course, Ingrid was thoroughly used to Rossellini's methods, but George Sanders proclaimed that he was utterly miserable throughout, had no idea what he was doing or why, and only afterwards, on reflection, thought that perhaps he might rather have enjoyed the experience.

Meanwhile, Ingrid and Rossellini had been working on something very different: a stage presentation of the opera-oratorio by Paul Claudel and Arthur Honegger *Joan of Arc at the Stake*. Naturally this held a great appeal for Ingrid, since it gave her another chance to get St Joan right. It was also a challenge for Rossellini to give visual interest and variety to what was essentially a very static, undramatic work. They decided from the first to ignore the original stage direction which has Joan tied to the stake, unmoving, throughout the just over an hour the piece runs: this, after all, was another adventure through the mind of a woman, and her mind runs free even if her body is in chains. There was also the opportunity to use all sorts of cinematic devices like back projection to enliven the bare, uncluttered stage. And it brought some unheralded tests for Ingrid along the way. Not only, in the course of the European tour, did she have to do it in five languages – Italian, Swedish, French, Spanish and English – but she had to conquer the objections of Claudel, by then a grand old man of letters, at their playing fast and loose with his original conception and, in Sweden, she had to face the most concentrated hostility and outright malice in her whole career.

This is hard to explain, but any Swede will tell you that it is deeply ingrained in the national character: whereas in France, say, any success a French performer has abroad only intensifies popularity at home, being felt to be all to the greater national glory, in Sweden any success a Swede may have outside the

Right. In Joan at the Stake *on stage.*

country is fiercely resented and dismissed – the very fact of leaving Sweden, if only temporarily, is regarded as some sort of betrayal. So when Ingrid and the *Joan of Arc* company arrived in Stockholm she was greeted with an almost incredible barrage of hostile press comment – she could literally do nothing right. Being the kind of person she was, she faced up to it all, quoting Strindberg: 'If I say No they beat me. If I say Yes, they beat me,' and went on with the show – to gratifyingly large audiences, even if they consisted to begin with largely of sensation-seekers.

After a while she got tired of accepting without answer attacks like the one which began by announcing that she never had been an actress, and now she was just a travelling freak show, exhibiting herself for money, and determined one evening to burn her boats by using an appearance at a charity benefit to make her reply from the stage. Everyone told her that if she did anything so crazy she would never be able to return to Sweden, but at this point she no longer cared. And in fact her speech, typically direct and guileless, seemed to arouse some latent sense of fair play in her audience and the press: from then on she was much better treated, and seemed after a fashion to have made her peace with Sweden. At the end of the tour, which also included Naples, Palermo, the Scala Milan, the Paris Opera, Barcelona and London, Rossellini recorded the production on film, though this version was very rarely shown.

In order to recoup, they went straight into a German-financed production, made in Munich and based on Stefan Zweig's novel *Der Angst*. It is another curious, intense psychological drama, about a bored married woman having a discreet affair who is first blackmailed then finds that her husband is organizing the blackmail. His motivation seems – it is not very clear – to force her into an explicit avowal of her infidelity, because only then will they be

Left. Radiant motherhood: Ingrid with Robertino and the twins, Ingrid and Isabella.

free to start again. Nowadays it looks like the best of the Rossellini/ Bergman films, with its superior technical qualities derived from more orderly German shooting methods. But at the time it was more mercilessly condemned by the critics than any of the others – most significantly by the Italian Angelo Solmi, who remarked on the half-a-dozen tries with negative results which proved 'the inability of the couple to create anything acceptable to the public or the critics' and concluded that they would 'either have to change their style of work radically – or retire into dignified silence.'

This was not, admittedly, the worst review they had ever had, but it did hit closest to the mark. Whether Rossellini had destroyed Ingrid's career, or she his, there could be little doubt that professionally they were not good for one another. Though Rossellini had made films without Ingrid during their association, she had done nothing without him, and he remained madly

Left. A portrait at the time of Angst. *Minerva.*

possessive about her, unwilling that she should ever work with another director again. It seemed like an impasse. But then two things happened. First, Jean Renoir, an old friend of Ingrid's, fulfilled a long-term promise to her by coming up with a film subject for her, and to her amazement and relief Rossellini agreed. And second, Rossellini himself had received an offer to make a documentary in India, and was busy arranging to do so, with the result that his vigilance and power over Ingrid were finally relaxing a little. If Ingrid's marriage to Petter had come to seem like a cage to her, so now her marriage to Rossellini felt much the same – though to be fair, while she had cast Petter in the role of jailer, the Rossellini marriage was a cage in which, she recognized, both were equally imprisoned, equally frustrated and chafing for release. The contract to make *Eléna et les Hommes* for Renoir in Paris was the key both Ingrid and Rossellini were unconsciously waiting for, and it must have been evident that once she had used it to escape she was never going to be manoeuvred right back into that particular cage again.

THE INTERNATIONAL YEARS

Eléna et les Hommes was intended as a frothy, lightweight comedy of intrigue about a silly woman who imagines herself as an éminence grise but cannot actually sustain the role. Even in France it had no great success, being regarded as, at best, very minor Renoir, while it was never shown in Britain and released in the States only in a dubbed, garbled version called *Paris Does Strange Things*. Nor was it by any stretch of the imagination a suitable role for Ingrid: while by no means lacking in humour, she never possessed that particular kind of light touch, and her performance tended to be leaden just when it should have lifted. But never mind: at least she was away from Rossellini, working on something completely different, and she was amazed how much she loved it, how much she had been missing for those last six years.

Rossellini made trouble, of course – in his usual histrionic fashion which made it difficult to know how seriously one should take him. If Ingrid did not do just what he wanted he might kidnap the children, or kill himself (he claimed to have picked out just the tree he was going to crash his car into). He was somewhat mollified when he was offered a play to direct in Paris, but then even further cast down when the leading actor refused to work with him and he was fired. But as compensation he was

Eléna et les Hommes (Paris Does Strange Things). *The men here are Mel Ferrer and Jean Marais. Warner Bros.*

offered another play, a French translation of *Tea and Sympathy*. And who knows, said the management disingenuously, perhaps your wife would care to take the female lead in it? Ingrid read the play and liked it, but foresaw problems. The matter had to be shelved for the moment, though, because something much more important came up: the chance to play in the film of *Anastasia*.

The play, an English version of a French original lightly fictionalizing the real-life case of Anna Anderson, who may or may not be the Grand-Duchess Anastasia, mysteriously survived from the massacre of the Romanov family during the Russian Revolution, had been bought for filming by Twentieth Century-Fox and was to be directed by Anatole Litvak. His only condition was that he wanted Ingrid or no one to play the role. Fox were terrified: maybe feeling was still so strong against her in the States that the picture would be boycotted. But Litvak was persistent, and secretly approached Ingrid to ask if she was interested provided 'they' could be persuaded. Was she? She recognized that the play, if not very profound, offered a succession of wonderful scenes that any actress would give her eye-teeth for. So she said yes, and then waited till Fox had also said yes (market research convinced them that they were not running such a terrible risk) before broaching the subject with Rossellini. Frenzies, scenes, dramas. But for once she was strong and determined. Apart from anything else, they desperately needed the money.

Anastasia was made in London, and the role might have been tailor-made for Ingrid. She is equally good at both ends of the *Pygmalion*-like progression Anastasia goes through, from the bedraggled amnesiac to the dazzling princess, and the 'big scene', when the claimant finally has to meet the dowager empress, her grandmother, is as played by Ingrid and Helen Hayes extremely touching. During the shooting Rossellini came to visit Ingrid once, a clear indication that all was not well with their marriage. Once the shooting was over and she returned to Paris, he was with her again, though again mainly for the melodramatic staging of grand guignol scenes. She wanted to do *Tea and Sympathy*; he absolutely did not. It was a terrible, disgusting play, he could not see any interest in anything even remotely connected with homosexuality, and she was definitely forbidden to do it. She did it anyway, scored a tremendous triumph with it, and he went off to India in a huff to make his documentary. It might have been just a necessary breathing-space, but the separation proved decisive. While she was received back, the prodigal daughter, with open arms by the American film industry, and got ever further away from the kind of films they had made together, stories started to filter back from India of his scandalous involvement with his Indian producer's wife. Well, good luck to him, thought Ingrid; and especially good luck to her, since now she will have to cope with all the storm and stress instead of me.

In any case, during the run of *Tea and Sympathy*, Ingrid also

Opposite. Anastasia discovered as a human wreck. 20th Century-Fox.

Below. Anastasia. The princess meets her grandmother (Helen Hayes). 20th Century-Fox.

had met someone else. A tall, handsome Swede called Lars Schmidt, who was coincidentally a successful theatrical producer, and, perhaps not so coincidentally, somewhat resembled Petter. They found immediately that they had a sense of humour in common and relaxed very well together – which must have been the most desirable quality in the world for Ingrid after her experience of the last few years. She was not sure whether she wanted to plunge again immediately into another marriage, but it seemed, all the same, that it would suit both her and Rossellini very well to get their Mexican marriage annulled. Nor should there be any great difficulty about that, unless someone made difficulties. Of course, Rossellini did. Even though he had his own reasons for wanting to be free, he saw no reason why sauce for the gander should be sauce for the goose: he announced that he wanted guarantees that Ingrid would never marry again, and that his children would never, ever visit America, even after they were fully adult. More seriously, he kept up a running battle about custody of the children, what religion they should be brought up in and so on, almost entirely, it seemed, for the sheer pleasure of the fight. The complications of legal detail in at least four countries mounted up so much that finally Ingrid did not know whether she was free to marry again or not. But by Christmas 1958 she and Lars were able to have a very quiet ceremony in London.

Before that all sorts of other things had happened. During the run of *Tea and Sympathy* it was announced that she had won her second Oscar, for *Anastasia*: in Hollywood's terms, her redemption from her fallen state could hardly be more convincingly demonstrated. She had already made her long-delayed return to the States – the occasion when she decided not to see Pia – in

Above. Ingrid leaving court during the legal battles with Rossellini for the custody of their children.

Right and below. Ingrid with awards for Anastasia.

January 1957, and found that few if any seemed to bear grudges against her; the New York Critics' Award for *Anastasia*, which she went personally to collect, proved in more than one way to presage the shape of things to come. And then, after *Tea and Sympathy* she had gone to London to film a light comedy, *Indiscreet*, with one of her favourite leading men, Cary Grant. A bit of nonsense about a perennial bachelor who preserves his status by pretending to have an undivorcible wife, and an actress he is romancing who determines to give him a dose of his own medicine, it was just the kind of thing Ingrid needed to lighten things up a bit, and if again she possibly enjoys herself too much on screen to be fully enjoyed by an audience, few have ever cared to grudge her this small measure of indulgence.

With her divorce from Rossellini finally confirmed and her marriage to Lars Schmidt achieved, Ingrid could at last settle into a steady professional routine with little or no history to be recounted. The public had forgiven and forgotten; she was just a big, big star who made films and stage appearances when she felt

Above. Indiscreet. *Warner Bros.*

Opposite. Indiscreet. *Top: on location with Cary Grant and director Stanley Donen and, below, sharing a joke in the film. Warner Bros.*

like it. Some of them were very successful, some less so – but that's the way things go in showbusiness. Even when, after seventeen years, she and Lars amicably parted and decided on divorce, no one noticed or cared – in fact for quite a while not even their closest friends knew that it had happened. At last she had found that closest earthly approximation to an ideal state where virtually the only external events of any importance in her life were the films and plays in which she appeared: her greatest joy had always been in her work, her greatest misery to be denied it. Mercifully, that did not happen any more: at a time of life which proves awkward for many actresses, around the fifties and early sixties, she was still playing leading roles, not just slipped in as somebody's mother, and if she did not always select her films very wisely, there was always the stage, where Lars called her the 'Golden Goose' because she never had a flop. Even in her final illness, she was able to work right to the end, longer than anyone, even she, thought possible.

Above and left. Ingrid with (above) her children by Rossellini and (below) with Pia.

*Above and right. Ingrid with her
third husband, Lars Schmidt, at an
Academy Award Presentation in
1959. Pia is on Ingrid's right in the
top photograph.*

Left. With Gunnar Björnstrand in
Stimulantia. *Omnia Film*.

During Ingrid's last twenty years there was, inevitably, a lot of
tying-up of loose ends. In 1967, for instance, after a nearly thirty
years' gap, she went back to work in a Swedish film, in Swedish:
it was an episode in a film called *Stimulantia*, based on the cruel
little Maupassant story about a couple whose whole lives are
ruined by the necessity to replace a valuable necklace the wife
borrows and loses – and, after ten years of penury, discovers was
only a worthless paste imitation after all. And the point was that
when the veteran Gustav Molander was asked to contribute to
the film, at the age of seventy-seven, he said he would come out
of retirement to do it only if Ingrid would star. That was quite an
emotional occasion.

It seems unlikely that Ingrid's final return to a Hollywood
studio the following year, to make *Cactus Flower* for Columbia,
can have set up quite so many vibrations: it was a good solid
comic role for a mature woman who has to be mousy and
glamorous by turns – and gets her man in the end, over some
more youthful opposition – and she probably thought no more
about doing it in Hollywood, after a twenty-year gap, then she
would if it had been made in London or Paris or Rome. Already
the new permissive morality, or at any rate a neat, publicity-
nurtured idea of it, had taken over Hollywood, and in a world
where film stars lived openly with their lovers and even had
children out of wedlock without the public turning a hair,
Ingrid's great transgression seemed light-years away. Indeed, it

was already a decade since the last star to shatter a prim, ladylike image by getting divorced, Deborah Kerr, had managed to cause even the smallest flutter of adverse comment, and even in 1957 the fuss already seemed rather cooked up and anachronistic. Whether for better or for worse, Hollywood in 1968 was not at all the same place as when Ingrid had left – any more than Washington was when a Senator Percy used her visit to the capital playing *Captain Brassbound's Conversion* in 1972 as an occasion to put the congressional record straight with a glowing testimonial intended to blot out for ever Senator Johnson's earlier denunciation.

The general impression one gets of this phase in her career is that she was not so enterprising in her choice of roles as one might expect from her vociferously expressed early ambitions. If we look at the record in detail, though, that does not seem to be true. It is simply that on the whole what we remember are the films and plays where she was, after all, playing very close to type, not those where she was, she felt, stretching her capabilities as an actress. *The Inn of the Sixth Happiness* (1958), for instance, where she plays Gladys Aylward, a dedicated British missionary in China, is not a particularly good film, stodgy and inclined to be mawkish, like a sort of Protestant *Bells of St Mary's* with exotic detailing. But we remember her in it, because when it comes to projecting uncomplicated goodness and transparent honesty there was no one to match her. (Ironically, in one respect she was

Opposite. The Inn of the Sixth Happiness. *20th Century-Fox*.

Cactus Flower. *Left: Loretta Young visits Ingrid on the set and, above, Ingrid with Goldie Hawn as rivals on the dance floor. Columbia.*

Left. On location in London as Gladys Aylward. 20th Century-Fox.

Opposite. In Aimez-vous Brahms? (Goodbye Again). *United Artists.*

Left. With Lars Schmidt at the premiere of The Inn of the Sixth Happiness. *20th Century-Fox.*

notably cast here against type: Gladys Aylward was, as the title
of the book on which the film was based indicates, famously a
'small woman'!) In *Goodbye Again* (1961), based on Françoise
Sagan's in its time mildly scandalous novel *Aimez-vous Brahms?*,
Ingrid plays a lightly ageing Paris decorator torn between two
loves, one her long-established and now fading affair with a man
of her own age (Yves Montand) and the other a more frantic
relationship with a boy (Anthony Perkins) she turns to out of
loneliness. In classic Hollywood days she would probably not
have been allowed (explicitly) to do more than 'date' either of
them, let alone have have sexual relations with both. But Ingrid is
still the Ingrid we have known and loved, suffering on both
counts and, in properly moral fashion, ending up with neither
man. Again, she is memorable, though the film is of little account.

But as well as these and others such, there were determined
attempts on her part to break new ground. They were just that
much less convincing. In *The Visit* (1964) she is called upon, even
in this drastically softened version of Dürrenmatt's savage stage
fable, to play an evil, heartless woman. We can certainly admire
her for wanting to try, but hardly have much good to say of the

Opposite top. Dancing with Anthony Perkins while her lover, Yves Montand, looks on in Aimez-vous Brahms? (Goodbye Again).
United Artists.
Opposite bottom. Ingrid with the journalists at the Cannes Film Festival in 1961. United Artists.

Right and overleaf. Big, bad Ingrid in The Visit. *20th Century-Fox.*

result. Likewise, however much she wanted to play Ibsen's classic heroine Hedda Gabler, for however long, Hedda's cruel, destructive edge eluded her, both on stage and on television. 'People don't do things like that,' observes the cynical Judge Brack after Hedda has shot herself. Well, not if they are Ingrid Bergman they don't, and we are never likely to believe the contrary, however determinedly we are told.

No doubt Ingrid just was not so bright or so perceptive about her own best career interests as she liked to think. It is not an

Left. In From the Mixed-up Files of Mrs Basil E. Frankweiler. *Cinema 5.*

uncommon failing with actors. She made films, for the best possible reasons, which were doomed from the outset. Indeed, two of her films of the 1970s, the oddly entitled *From the Mixed-Up Files of Mrs Basil E. Frankweiler* and Vincente Minnelli's Rome-made *A Matter of Time*, in which she plays (not very convincingly, being much too sensible for the role) a dotty old countess once loved by all the artists and crowned heads of Europe, were never properly released and seen by almost nobody. But she also got a third Oscar in 1975, this time for a supporting role in a film of supporting roles, Agatha Christie's ingenious whodunit *Murder on the Orient Express*, and that was through following out her own instinct: when Sidney Lumet offered her the role of a fabulous old Russian princess on board she begged him to let her play the drab and rather crazed Swedish missionary instead. And there were the vastly successful stage appearances in 'light classics' such as *Captain Brassbound's Conversion*, Maugham's *The Constant Wife* and finally N.C. Hunter's *Waters of the Moon*, where she and Wendy Hiller played the roles first played by Dame Edith Evans and Dame Sybil Thorndike, and did not suffer by the inevitable comparison.

And above all there was *Autumn Sonata*. Is that a case of the exception that proves the rule, the star for once doing wonders when cast completely against type? Possibly. But though Ingrid claimed she could not understand the character, could not con-

Opposite. Portrait from The Yellow Rolls Royce. *MGM.*

Above. Ingrid and Ingmar Bergman on the set of Autumn Sonata. *New World Pictures.*

ceive how any mother could behave like that, she surely could. Not in specifics, of course, but in a general sort of a way, it could be seen as her story exactly. Like the pianist in *Autumn Sonata* she was always self-willed, self-centred, driven more surely and consistently by the necessities of her career than anything else. Certainly she was not always happy in it, but her major happiness and fulfilment always came from acting – the only area where she could follow the dictates of her heart with a clear conscience and no lingering guilt the morning after. This was obviously why her association with Rossellini could not last: it did not work professionally, and without that nothing else could be enough for very long. This was no doubt the root cause that two of her husbands abandoned her, one of the most beautiful and desirable women in the world, and that she was endlessly at loggerheads with her children, one at a time or all at once.

No, if she was honest with herself the character in *Autumn Sonata* was no stranger to her – though needless to say it was the special genius of Ingmar Bergman and the special working relationship between them that compelled or tricked her into such a vivid piece of soulsearching. And then, she still had a few tricks of her own up her sleeve – as a star, as an actress and, one is tempted to say, as a woman. She did not seem to think so. After *Autumn Sonata* on film and *Waters of the Moon* on stage, she frequently said that she did not think she would perform again. But she always said it with regret, so it was not such a surprise when, though she was rumoured to be very ill, it was announced that she would, after all, make another film. But the film itself was very surprising: in *A Woman Called Golda*, a two-part film for television, she was going to play a character who could hardly, one would have said, be farther away from her in appearance, background and character: none other than the late great Prime Minister of Israel, Golda Meir.

The prospect, truth to tell, created almost as much alarm as delight in Ingrid's fans. They need not have worried. True, the script is conceived in terms of popular hagiography (Golda Meir as a real-life modern Joan of Arc, perhaps?), and everything is so smotheringly warm and wonderful that one longs for something really abrasive to scrape away the sugar-coating. On earlier showing Ingrid would hardly have seemed the person to do it. Of course her brisk, no-nonsense approach to life (at any rate life on screen) could help a lot, but it somehow did not seem quite what the character of Golda Meir or an over-reverential film about her needed. Nor, miraculously, was that what they got. One keeps saying that Ingrid was a star first and foremost. That does not preclude acting ability, but does tend to render it largely irrelevant. Ingrid had always maintained she could act, if given a chance. Here, almost perversely – or perhaps because it was the only real challenge left – she set out to prove it. Of course you always know, somewhere at the back of your mind, that this is Ingrid Bergman you are watching. But, for the first time in Ingrid's whole career, you know but often do not remember. From the voice – the timbre of someone who regularly smoked three packs of cigarettes a day, the accent of a Russian Jew brought up in New York – the character is built so surely and confidently that the performance is what counts most, not who precisely is giving it.

All the same, there are odd echoes for those alert to them. Golda was a woman who gave up everything – husband, children, the possibility of a happy second marriage, the comfortable retirement her incurable illness seemed to require of her – for a career. True, the career was the bringing to birth and preservation of the state of Israel, a lofty enough ideal in all conscience. But we are left in little doubt that the ideal came from a personal imperative of her own temperament: in a way, devoting herself wholly to the cause was the most selfish thing Golda could do. In many ways the same was uncomfortably true of Ingrid. Her ideal was acting, or at any rate performing. However much it might seem like drudgery, she was happy in it; nothing – and nobody – else would suffice. Hence, perhaps because of what she had learned of her own potential, the way other people might see her life, from *Autumn Sonata*, Ingrid managed, in *A Woman Called Golda*, to triumph over a sloppy conception and give one of the most extraordinary performances of her life.

There was another point of identification too. In the scene where Golda is told she has an incurable disease of a cancerous

type, there is an extraordinary intensity which must owe something to an audience's awareness that Ingrid has faced the same problem, to an anecdotal curiosity about what she is thinking as she plays the scene. But it is not, one would swear, just that. Whatever she is thinking and feeling, like whatever John Wayne was thinking and feeling when he played the fatally ill gunfighter in his last film, *The Shootist*, shines out from the screen without need of explanation and footnotes: it is something a spectator who had never before heard of Ingrid Bergman and knew nothing of her personal circumstances would surely feel too. It was an extraordinary farewell, by a woman very close to death: she did not even live long enough to collect her well-deserved Emmy.

For all the ups and downs, either of which might have destroyed a lesser person, she had had a good life and, especially in what concerned her work and raison d'être, an amazingly long and productive life. She was not, perhaps, especially gifted in self-knowledge: even in *My Story*, the semi-autobiography she wrote with Alan Burgess, author of *The Small Woman*, two years before her death, the point of view is defiantly her own, and though she good-humouredly recounts the major mistakes of her life, she never seems to to learn from them. But then, self-knowledge is a two-edged weapon for artists: if they know too clearly what it is that drives them onward, the drive itself may slacken and fail. According to her lights, Ingrid was a good woman, and a strong woman. Even without knowing where the various phases in her life might lead her, she made her way with the certainty of a sleepwalker, and bravely accepted responsibility for her own actions. When the inevitability of her death from cancer became evident, she accepted that too, with extraordinary courage and an unbreakable will to continue. She was an actress, and a good one, as she proved never more effectively than in her very last films.

But more than that, whatever she chose to think, she was a star: her great emotional relationship was with the camera, and that was that. We remember her – we want to remember her – not acting away pretending to be a Spanish peasant or a nicely rowdy nun, but at that moment when she did not know who she was or whom she was supposed to love or why. It did not matter: it was enough just that she stroll across the screen while 'Play it again, Sam' was still echoing in our minds and hearts. Strange the potency of cheap music and priceless stars . . .